WE ANIMALS

Poems of Our World

EDITED AND WITH ESSAYS BY

Nadya Aisenberg

Sierra Club Books
San Francisco

Library of Congress Cataloging-in-Publication Data
We Animals : poems of our world / edited and with essays by Nadya Aisenberg.
p.   cm.
Bibliography: p. 195
ISBN 0-87156-679-6
0-87156-685-0 pbk.
1. Animals—Poetry.   I. Aisenberg, Nadya.
PN6110.A7W4   1989
808.81'936—dc19   88-35043
CIP

Frontispiece: "The Animal Kingdom," cut paper
and watercolor, Massachusetts, c.1825–1850.

Jacket/cover design by Bonnie Smetts
Book design by Abigail Johnston

Printed in the United States of America
10 9 8 7 6 5 4 3 2 1

Acknowledgments

I would like to acknowledge with gratitude the generous help of many friends and colleagues who read portions or earlier drafts of this book in manuscript: Marilyn Brownstein, Naomi Chase, Miriam Goodman, Mona Harrington, Louise Kawada, Marion Mainwaring, Cornelia Veenendaal. For specific suggestions about poems, I would like to thank Marjorie Agosin, Kate Barnes, and especially Sue Standing; Dr. Leon Weiss contributed enthusiasm and confidence in the project; and Susan Werbe provided intelligent and conscientious library assistance. Finally, I am indebted to Marie Cantlon, who encouraged and guided me in the early stages of the project and brought her valuable editorial judgment to the book as it took shape, and to Daniel Moses of Sierra Club Books.

I would also like to express my thanks to The National Endowment for the Humanities for a Stipend received at the outset of this project, to The Virginia Center for the Creative Arts for a residency in January 1987 when some of this book was written, and to the following publishers.

"Never Again Would Birds' Song Be the Same," © 1942 by Robert Frost and renewed 1970 by Leslie Frost Ballantine. Reprinted from *The Poetry of Robert Frost*, edited by Edward Connery Lathem, by permission of Henry Holt and Company, Inc.

"The Heavy Bear," *New and Selected Poems 1938–1958*, by Delmore Schwartz, reprinted by permission of Doubleday & Co., 1959.

"The Bat," © 1938 by Theodore Roethke. From the *Collected Poems of Theodore Roethke*, reprinted by permission of Doubleday, a division of Bantam, Doubleday, Dell Publishing Group, Inc.

"Animals," *Selected Poems* of Robinson Jeffers, reprinted by permission of Vintage Books, 1965.

"Teaching the Ape to Write," *Absences: New Poems,* © 1970 by James Tate, reprinted by permission of Little, Brown, Atlantic Monthly Books.

"Giant Panda," Kabiru Abdu Kila, *Summer Fires: New Poetry of Africa,* reprinted by permission of Heinemann, London, 1983.

"A Dog Asleep on My Feet," *Poems 1957–67,* by James Dickey, reprinted by permission of Wesleyan University Press.

"Horses," by Murilo Mendes, *Twentieth-Century Brazilian Literature,* edited and with introduction by Elizabeth Bishop and Emanuel Brasil. Reprinted by permission of Wesleyan University Press, 1972.

"Sonnet of Intimacy," by Vinícius de Moraes, *Twentieth-Century Brazilian Literature,* edited and with introduction by Elizabeth Bishop and Emanuel Brasil. Reprinted by permission of Wesleyan University Press, 1972.

"Two Horses Playing in the Orchard," *Collected Poems,* by James Wright, reprinted by permission of Wesleyan University Press, 1971.

"Animals Are Passing from Our Lives," *Not This Pig,* by Philip Levine, reprinted by permission of Wesleyan University Press, 1968.

"Caring for Animals," *Poems New and Selected,* by Jon Silkin, reprinted by permission of Wesleyan University Press, 1986.

"Shooting Whales," *Selected Poems of Mark Strand,* reprinted by permission of Atheneum Publishers, 1980.

"In Monument Valley," *From the First Nine,* by James Merrill, reprinted by permission of Atheneum Publishers, 1984.

"St. Francis and the Sow," *Mortal Acts, Mortal Words,* by Galway Kinnell, © 1980 by Galway Kinnell. Reprinted by permission of Houghton Mifflin.

"Swan Song," *Red Coal,* by Gerald Stern, Houghton Mifflin, 1981; © Gerald Stern, reprinted by permission of the author.

"The Man-Moth," *The Complete Poems 1927–1979* of Elizabeth Bishop. Reprinted by permission of Farrar, Straus and Giroux, 1987.

"#XXXIX," *Midsummer,* by Derek Walcott, reprinted by permission of Farrar, Straus and Giroux, 1984.

"The Season of Phantasmal Peace," by Derek Walcott, *The Fortunate Traveller,* reprinted by permission of Farrar, Straus and Giroux, 1981.

"The Bull Returns," *Selected Poetry of Yehuda Amichai,* reprinted by permission of Harper & Row, 1986.

"Second Glance at a Jaguar," *Selected Poems* of Ted Hughes, reprinted by permission of Harper & Row, 1972.

"Little Elegy with Books and Beasts," reprinted by permission; © 1987 Nancy Willard. Originally in *The New Yorker.*

"An Ox Looks at Man," by Carlos Drummond de Andrade; "The Emu and the Nobilities of Interest," by Les A. Murray; reprinted by permission of *The New Yorker* magazine.

"The Snake," *The Complete Poems of D. H. Lawrence,* reprinted by permission of Viking Press, 1964.

"The Lion in Love," *The Complete Poems of Marianne Moore,* reprinted by permission of the Macmillan Co./Viking Press, 1967.

"Dreamscapes"; "Creatures," by Philip Booth. *Relations: Selected Poems 1950–1985,* reprinted by permission of Viking/Penguin, 1986.

"How It Goes On," *Our Ground Time Here Will Be Brief,* by Maxine Kumin, © 1976 by Maxine Kumin. All rights reserved. Reprinted by permission of Viking Penguin, Inc.

"Materialized into an Owl," by Louis (Little Coon) Oliver, *Songs from This Earth on Turtle's Back: Contemporary American Indian Poetry,* reprinted by permission of Greenfield Review Press, 1983.

"Monkeys at Hardwar," by Taufiq Rafat, *Aftermath: An Anthology of Poems in English from Africa,* reprinted by permission of Greenfield Review Press, 1977.

"Sonnets to Orpheus: Second Part, IV," by Rainer Maria Rilke, *Sonnets to Orpheus,* translated by Stephen Mitchell. Reprinted by permission of Simon and Schuster, 1985.

"Cleopatra," *Portrait of a Nude Woman As Cleopatra,* by Barbara Chase-Riboud, reprinted by permission of William Morrow, 1987.

"The Chance to Love Everything," *Dream Work,* by Mary Oliver, reprinted by permission of Atlantic Monthly Press, 1986.

"Gnat-Psalm," *Woodwo,* by Ted Hughes, reprinted by permission of Faber & Faber, 1967.

"With Trumpets and Zithers," *Selected Poems of Czeslaw Milosz,* reprinted by permission of Ecco Press, 1980.

"From March '79," *Selected Poems of Tomas Tranströmer 1954–1986,* Ecco Press, 1987.

"Homesickness," *Selected Poems of Marina Tsvetayeva,* reprinted by permission of E. P. Dutton, 1986, and Century Hutchinson Publishing Group, Ltd., London.

"The Origin of Centaurs," *The Hard Hours,* by Anthony Hecht, reprinted by permission of Atheneum Publishers, 1967.

"Adam's Task," *The Night Mirror,* by John Hollander, reprinted by permission of Atheneum Publishers, 1971.

"The Horses of Achilles," *The Complete Poems of Cavafy,* reprinted by permission of Harcourt Brace Jovanovich, 1974.

"The Peace of Wild Things," *Openings,* by Wendell Berry, reprinted by permission of Harcourt, Brace & World, 1968.

"Beasts," *New and Collected Poems by Richard Wilbur,* reprinted by permission of Harcourt Brace Jovanovich, 1988.

"Words Rising," by Robert Bly, from *The Man in the Black Coat Turns,* © Robert Bly. Reprinted by permission of Doubleday & Co., 1988.

"The Spider," by César Vallejo, from *Selected Poems of Vallejo and Neruda,* translated by Robert Bly, John Knoepfle, and James Wright, Beacon Press, 1970; © Robert Bly 1970. Reprinted with his permission.

"Some Beasts," by Pablo Neruda, from *Selected Poems of Vallejo and Neruda,* translated by Robert Bly, John Knoepfle, and James Wright, Beacon Press, 1970; © Robert Bly 1970. Reprinted with his permission.

"Calling In the Hawk," from *Ridge Music,* by Harry Humes, University of Arkansas Press, 1987. Reprinted by permission of the author.

"The Grove," *Collected Poems by Edwin Muir,* © 1960 by Willa Muir. Reprinted by permission of Oxford University Press, Inc.

"Zoo Gardens Revisited," *Second Sight,* by A. K. Ramanujan, reprinted by permission of Oxford University Press, 1986.

"Hymn to the Spirit of the Air," by Igpakuhak; "The Song of the Trout-Fisher," by Ikinilik, *Eskimo Poems from Canada and Greenland,* edited by Tom Lowenstein, reprinted by permission of University of Pittsburgh Press, © Tom Lowenstein, 1973.

"Come into Animal Presence," *Jacob's Ladder,* by Denise Levertov, reprinted by permission of New Directions, 1961.

"The Sea-Elephant," *Collected Poems, Volume I: 1909–1939,* by William Carlos Williams, © 1938 by New Directions Publishing Corporation.

"Flame, Speech," *Selected Poems of Octavio Paz,* reprinted by permission of New Directions, 1984.

"Mother Earth: Her Whales," *Turtle Island,* by Gary Snyder, reprinted by permission of New Directions, 1969.

"A Difference of Zoos," *Long Live Man,* by Gregory Corso, reprinted by permission of New Directions, 1962.

"If the Owl Calls Again," *Winter News,* by John Haines, reprinted by permission of Wesleyan University Press, 1962.

"The Second Coming," *Selected Poems and Two Plays of William Butler Yeats,* reprinted by permission of Macmillan Publishing Co., 1962.

"The Oxen," *The Complete Poems of Thomas Hardy,* reprinted by permission of Macmillan Publishing Co., 1976.

"The Lioness," *The Dream of a Common Language,* by Adrienne Rich, reprinted by permission of W. W. Norton, 1978.

"Easter Morning," *A Coast of Trees,* by A. R. Ammons, reprinted by permission of W. W. Norton, 1981.

"Less and Less Human, O Savage Spirit," *The Collected Poems of Wallace Stevens,* reprinted by permission of Random House, 1947.

"Leviathan: Physiologus: Chapters for a Bestiary," *Green with Beasts,* by W. S. Merwin, Alfred A. Knopf, 1956. Reprinted by permission of Rupert Hart-Davis Ltd., London.

"Original Sin: Part of a Short Story," *Selected Poems, 1923–1975,* © Robert Penn Warren. Reprinted by permission of Random House.

"The Sabbath," *W. H. Auden: Collected Poems,* reprinted by permission of Random House, 1977.

"Eighth Elegy," *Duino Elegies and Sonnets to Orpheus,* by Rainer Maria Rilke, translated by A. Poulin, Jr. Reprinted by permission of Random House, 1982.

"To the Maker of 'A Peaceable Kingdom,'" *Brotherly Love: A Poem,* by Daniel Hoffman, Random House, 1981; © Daniel Hoffman. Reprinted by permission of the author.

"The Elephant," by Carlos Drummond de Andrade, *Travelling in the Family: Selected Poems,* edited by Thomas Colchie and Mark Strand. Reprinted by permission of Random House, 1986.

"Death Is an Animal," by Violeta Parra, *The Renewal of the Vision,* edited by Marjorie Agosin and Cola Franken, reprinted by permission of Spectacular Diseases Press, Peterborough, England.

"There Are Things to Be Said," *In Good Time,* by Cid Corman, reprinted by permission of the author.

"The Unicorn, the Gorgon, and the Manticore," by Gian Carlo Menotti, reprinted by permission of G. Ricordi & Co., 1956.

"Mount Fuji, Opus 5," by Kusano Shimpei, *The Penguin Book of Japanese Verse,* translated by Geoffry Bownas and Anthony Thwaite, 1964.

"Dreamtigers," *Dreamtigers,* by Jorge Luis Borges, translated by Harold Morland and Mildred Boyer, University of Texas Press, Austin, Texas, 1964.

"The Leopard-Nurser," *The Chinese Insomniacs: New Poems,* by Josephine Jacobsen, reprinted by permission of University of Pennsylvania Press, 1981.

"The Beast," *The Good Thief,* by Marie Howe, reprinted by permission of Persea Books, New York, 1988.

"Saaka Crested Cranes," by David Rubadiri, *Aftermath: An Anthology of Poems in English from Africa, Asia, and the Caribbean,* edited by Roger Weaver and Joseph Bruhac, reprinted by permission of Greenfield Review Press, 1977.

"Adam Naming the Creatures," by Suzanne Berger, reprinted by permission of the author. This poem originally was published in the Sotheby International Poetry Competition 1982, London, and subsequently appeared in *Legacies,* by Suzanne Berger, Alice James Books, Cambridge, MA, 1984.

Illustration Acknowledgments:

"The Animal Kingdom," cut paper and watercolor, Massachusetts, c.1825–1850. Courtesy of National Gallery of Art, Washington, D.C. [Frontispiece]

Barque with Lion Goddess 1985, 6 foot processional, maximum height 16½ inches, by Ann McCoy. [Reverence]

Needlework Picture, Mary Upelbe, Massachusetts, 1767, courtesy of Historic Deerfield, Massachusetts. [Dominion]

"Animals Are Only Human (a group of mummers)," courtesy of Bodleian Museum, Oxford University, England. [Fraternity]

"Who Were The First To Cry Nowell?" woodcut by Eric Gill, courtesy of Museum of Fine Arts, Boston, Massachusetts. [Communion]

"Flying Tiger," Chinese, nineteenth century, courtesy of Metropolitan Museum of Art, N.Y., N.Y. [Fantasy]

CONTENTS

INTRODUCTION
2

REVERENCE
9

DOMINION
51

FRATERNITY
95

COMMUNION
137

FANTASY
167

CONCLUSION
190

Notes
192

Bibliography
195

Index to Poems
199

WE
ANIMALS

INTRODUCTION

Fewer men than ever flick reins across teams of oxen or dip nets for herring, yet human beings retain and carry forward an intimate and imaginative relationship with animals. Our perceptions of ourselves and what we survey, expressed in the creations of our imagination, acknowledge everywhere a profound sense of connectedness to other creatures.

Animal imagery crosses boundaries of history, geography, and cultural difference, surrounding us with evidence of these connections. Pagan myths invoking animals emphasize their power and ferocity, which play important roles in works such as *The Bacchae* and *The Odyssey;* early Judeo-Christian myths of the ingathering of people and animals in the Garden of Eden and Noah's Ark embody a vision of harmony and benignity. Animal imagery is central to the creation myths of the Orinoco Basin and to those of the Indus Valley, continents apart. In representational art, horses appear in paleolithic cave drawings at Lascaux and Altamira, as well as in the twentieth-century sculpture of Marini and Calder. Sea mammals are evoked in the Book of Job and in a recent poem, "The Seal," by Robert Bly. We use animals to demarcate the passage of time and our sense of ourselves as temporal beings: each year of the Chinese calendar is characterized by an animal symbol; eight of the twelve monthly signs of the zodiac are represented by animals; and each of the twelve hourly divisions of the Greek day is represented by an animal. Armorial bearings with animal blazons were intended to identify a household with some extraordinary powers of the adopted animal, say, the lion and the unicorn of Great Britain.

Blake's eighteenth-century poems about lambs and tygers approach animals in the same symbolic way that Picasso did to design a dove of peace as the official logo of the United Nations. And the fabulous beasts that decorate the tapestries at Cluny, or the strange hybrid animals that stalk Piero del Cosimo's painting "The Forest Fire," are examples of our perennial delight in creating fantastic animals. These examples, and countless others, exhibit the varied and complex relationships with animals we have represented through art. Both variety and complexity are present because animals serve as unique metaphors — they are capable of standing for us and yet remaining "other." They are, in the words of American naturalist John Muir, our "horizontal brothers" — another, but closely related.

Contemporary poetry reveals also with great richness how human/animal relationships continue to function for us now, demonstrating that our bonds with animals are an imaginative constant sustained in each age regardless of changing external conditions. Though our insights about these relationships may change, the presence and validity of the relationships are not called into question. And, indeed, the poems included in this book represent the merest sampling of the great wealth and diversity of poetry about animals being written today all over the world.

Contemporary poetry discloses three timeless and essential relationships: reverence, dominion, fraternity. A fourth, communion, introduces the more recent speculative and complicated issue of verbal and nonverbal communication as it applies to our exploration of species relationship. The last, fantasy, conjures with creatures of our own imagining. We find in the very existence of all this material that contemporary poets, like earlier ones, feel the necessity to "come into animal presence," as Denise Levertov phrases it. Their poems supply something we miss that we may not even have articulated for ourselves.

Today, we have fresh grounds for reaffirming ancient ties. Ushering in the modern period, Darwin and Freud provided us with biological and psychological findings refuting the position of speciesism, that is, the view that each species is subject to its own laws of nature and would most profitably be studied discretely. More recently, scientists such as Konrad Lorenz, Stephen Jay Gould, and Edmund O. Wilson, through their explorations of the social organization and modes of communication employed by other creatures, have brought new challenges to speciesism. At the very time, however, that the fledgling sciences of biosociology and zöosemiotics make us more knowledgeable about connections among species, about animal life and its importance for us, widespread pollution of air and water, coupled with the sprawl of concrete jungle from city to city (discussed in such cautionary books as *The Malling of America*[1]) have alerted us to the consequences of our despoliation of the natural environment. Most alarming, the extinction in living memory of many species and the depleted numbers of many more have made us anticipate an imminent and irreversible loss. One-fourth of the world's species are in danger of extinction in the next twenty years, warns Peter H. Raven, director of the Missouri Botanical Gardens.

We find ourselves unwilling to inhabit the universe alone. This is hardly surprising since, whether one looks to religious or scientific accounts of creation, animals were present before humans. Animals have inhabited a world without people, but people have *never* lived without the companionship, example, and practical help of animals. References to animals are so centrally fixed in our imagination and language, as well as in our visual iconography (the earliest known man-made images of animals date to nearly 30,000 years ago), that we cannot project a world without them. This, more than anything else, places in perspective our own briefer tenure on the planet.

Whereas in earlier times we interpreted the world through the lens of faith—whether as polytheists, believing that natural forces such as thunder, rain, moon, sun were godheads, that natural objects such as rocks and trees possessed a soul; or as monotheists, viewing creation as a spiritual text from whose presence the existence of a Creator could be deduced—in our own time the sustained effort to demythologize the universe has resulted in a general conviction that creation lacks inherent purpose. Analysis has replaced synthesis; our world lacks coherence. Perceiving a lack of order about us, we can no longer interpret nature as part of the evidence for a grand design. With ease and sweeping motions, we alter the nature we see around us, and our own domination robs it of a sacramental sense. Furthermore, the rapidity of change in the modern world, examined in Alvin Toffler's *Future Shock*,[2] means that we must constantly reassemble and reread the signs of the universe; it is no longer an open book. As a result, though our scientific understanding of the world has increased, the overall effect of scientific and technological progress has been to diminish our instinctual, emotional identification with nature. As things are, we feel isolated in our universe; Wordsworth laments for all of us, "Little we see in Nature that is ours." This loss has impelled us to a renewed interest in and respect for what links us to the natural world. Against our twentieth-century loss of belief, the poetry we can summon here counters our feeling of remoteness from nature by bringing the spiritual freshness of pastoral and wilderness before us again; these poems counter our isolation by insisting upon a historic, unbroken association with animals, thus enlarging our vision of ourselves in creation; and they render the experience of our lives more bearable by teaching us, through comparison with other creatures, something about our own divided selves.

Barque with Lion Goddess processional,
by Ann McCoy, 1985.

REVERENCE

My only final friends —

the wren and thrush, made solid print for me

across dawn's broken arc. No; yes . . . or were they

the audible ransom, ensign of my faith

towards something far, now further than ever away?

"A POSTSCRIPT"

HART CRANE

Humankind has gazed at animals with awe from pre-Biblical times to the present day. Looking back, we may think immediately of the zöomorphic deities of the Egyptians — cow-headed Hathor, goddess of love; wolf-headed Anubis, god of alchemy and astronomy — the Chinese dragon; the Mayan jaguar; the Celtic bull; the Minoan snake. Archaic peoples observed the ways in which animals surpassed human capacities and power and made of animals totems, tribal symbols, and even gods. Within historical time, cartographers inscribed "Monsters" on maps; people believed that mermaids existed, and were fearful of their seductive power. Furthermore, in the non-European world, the creation myths among South American Indians, Africans, Eskimos, and Hindus describe humanity's birth from an animal source — snake or turtle or raven — inextricably linking our own existence to the existence of animal deities from whom we descend. Perhaps our knowledge that animals existed before us makes them our first gods, as psychologist James Hillman suggests. Thus, Australian aborigines divide themselves into totemic clans based on their holy animal ancestor—Great Kangaroo, Great Lizard, Emu, Honey-ant, and so on. Though animal worship no longer prevails worldwide, much of the symbology and reverential attitude persist; we have only to think of the great winged lion of Saint Mark in the central piazza of Venice. And it is, of course, partially the symbolic view that implants other creatures in the human imagination forever. So D. H. Lawrence calls "Snake" a "god," "king," and "lord"; A. R. Ammons describes the "majesty" of soaring eagles; and Denise Levertov terms animal presence "holy presence."

For the Westerner in the twentieth century, it was the Romantic movement of the preceding century, with its swing from reason to feeling, its attraction to grandeur, wildness, heightened emotion, isolation, and primitivism, that both in painting and in poetry reinvigorated an attitude of reverence toward nature. The paintings of Cole, Church, Bierstadt, Delacroix, and Géricault exemplify this, finding correspondence in poems such as Byron's "Manfred," Blake's "Tyger, Tyger," Coleridge's "Christabel," and Wordsworth's "Prelude," to cite but a few among scores. During the same period, the discovery by the great westward explorations of virgin wilderness in America contributed to a sense of wonder; Washington Irving, for instance, called the American West "a natural church." In New England, Thoreau wrote, "I long for wildness . . . everlasting and unfallen." Wonder in the face of natural phenomena concentrates most strongly upon animals, for though we may travel to gaze on such sights as Victoria Falls or the redwood forest, the most powerful bonding is between man and animals. Today, emotions far deeper than nostalgia for a bygone wilderness, where, in fact, most of us have never dwelt, must explain the enormous audience commanded by public television programs such as "Nova," "Smithsonian World," "National Geographic," and "Wild America."

We regret the passing of something we never knew because the abolition of wilderness diminishes us, placing us in a less wondrous context, children only of our own urban jungles. Animals feel at home in the wilderness. When they are gone, from whom will we learn about a past that did not transpire in cities? In Philip Booth's "Dreamscape," this sentiment informs the last two stanzas:

> But when I sleep
> the left side of the blacktop
> clears itself into good pasture.
> There are two old horses,
> tethered. And a curving row
> of miniature bison, kneeling
>
> each with his two front hooves
> tucked in neatly under the lip
> of the asphalt. I am asleep.
> I cannot explain it. I do not
> want to explain it.

In much the same way, the passing of many so-called primitive human cultures from the world deprives us of knowing, seeing, feeling, moving, and understanding in totally unaccustomed ways. Although we tend to see in the march of time a proper evolutionary progress of civilizations, in fact extinction brings loss of both continuity and alternativeness.

Disney World's remarkable popularity with adults as well as children threatens to replace wonder by stripping animal life of its wildness, removing it from a natural setting, and rendering it impotent and cute/childish. These animals, like those in animated films from whence they came, are more than domesticated. They belong with infants, whom we find simultaneously appealing and unequal, and are rightfully condescended to by spectators, just as infants are. In such a denatured world, animals are made into objects, much like the tools which have superseded them. Such a view of creation has latent within it the ultimate horror — that we, too, like our animal kin, are part of a mechanistic cosmos, simply sentient cogs and wheels. Contemporary poems of reverence provide a vital counterpoise to this destructive pop culture, rescuing animals for a sacramental rather than a commercial and imaginatively reductive purpose. Do we think that by transforming animals into completely manageable puppets we can thereby deny or control the wildness and ferocity, ignore the appetites of our own natures? This is comparable to our scorn for "primitive" civilizations, which we disparage as more violent than ours. Even for children, these can only be misleading assumptions.

The poems centered on reverence illustrate three recurrent qualities for which animals are deified: freedom, superhuman prowess, and integrity.

Animal freedom can be identified as both the freedom from guilt and the freedom from the foreknowledge of mortality. The freedom from guilt means that animals enjoy a lack of self-consciousness; in their natural habitat they live openly with physical delight, exercising the sensual pleasure of the present moment, unrestrained by our laws, conventions, religions, all the inhibitions of conscience. For the most part, we vicariously enjoy their recapturing this libidinal energy for us. Both Walt Whitman in the poem "Animals" and William Carlos Williams in "The Sea-Elephant" praise animal freedom from the pangs of conscience, self-reproach, and anxiety. As critic Helen Vendler notes, "Those who want the perfect, if deprived of God, turn oddly often to the world of animals, who, since they cannot be other than they are, are therefore helplessly perfect."[1] Because they are perceived as living outside the terms of guilt, contemporary poetry commonly elevates them to a state of purity and innocence. The malaise defined by Descartes as the split between body and soul is absent in the animal, and it is therefore a comfort and a healing for both poet and reader to imagine animals and reflect upon them. Anthropologist Claude Lévi-Strauss makes the interesting observation that among hunting peoples an animal is held in totemic regard not only because it is good to eat, but because it is "good to think," that is, to hold in the imagination.[2]

Importantly, as the Twenty-third Psalm states, we human beings live "in the shadow of death," but animals have no such grievous anticipation. This is the second "major freedom," as

Richard Wilbur terms it in "Beasts," for which we envy the animals. The punishment of mortality that befell us after the expulsion from Eden is painful only because of our conscious expectation of it. (How painful this knowledge is can be inferred from our profound devotion to the compensatory idea of an afterlife, demonstrated by the custom, dating to antiquity, of elaborate funerary interments of food, clothing, jewels, and utensils to be used by the departed in the next world.) Moreover, because animals live only in the present, they have "no history to daunt them," as W. H. Auden points out,[3] whereas our own human infamies are part of the record of our race. Freed equally, then, from memory of past guilt and foretaste of future loss, animals seem to live on a plane of atemporality. Jorge Luis Borges remarks to his cat: "You live in other time / lord of your realm." And Mark Van Doren, reflecting upon the animals in the Ark, asks: "Did they lie sleeping patiently, as no man did, patiently? / ... They did not know the flow of time, they did not count the waves."

We may also attach a divinity to animals because, as they are delivered from our bondage to time, we grant them both an individual and a generic life, life in a particular time and an eternal time. As cultural historian John Berger comments, "An animal's blood flowed like human blood, but its species was undying and each lion was Lion, and each ox was Ox."[4] We perceive animals as existing in a timeless dimension similar to other natural forces such as sea and wind, or to the immutable figures on Keats's Grecian vase. The snake in the ritual mysteries at Eleusis fulfilled its function because it was "snake," not a particular snake; in Arabia the bull symbolizes the moon, which may wax and wane but whose latent strength is always there. Borges in his poem "To the Nightingale" cites Virgil, the Persian poets, Shakespeare, Heine, Keats, "the Muslim," all of whom have contributed to the nightingale's immortal (timeless) voice "in exultation, memory and fable," until Borges declares: "Perhaps I never heard you, but my life / is bound up with your life, inseparably." We are linked culturally to symbols whose meaning accrues throughout history, and this is one way we transcend our own prescribed compass of time.

The mythic vision of animals existing outside the human framework of days underlies and empowers such diverse works as Rudyard Kipling's *The Jungle Book* and W. B. Yeats's poem "The Wild Swans at Coole." The Irish poet contrasts his own mutability, "All's changed . . . " with his vision of the wild, unaging swans on the lake at Coole:

> Unwearied still, lover by lover,
> They paddle in the cold
> Companionable streams or climb the air;
> Their hearts have not grown old.

More recently Italian poet Eugenio Montale restated this same idea of animal time as both individual and generic: "A blackbird and even a dog dead for years, can perhaps return since for ourselves they matter more as 'species' than as individuals." That is, the individual animal's life is less important than the continuation of the species in its symbolic power, which is what renders possible James Dickey's vision of resurrection in the last stanza of "The Heaven of Animals":

> At the cycle's center,
> They tremble, they walk
> Under the tree,
> They fall, they are torn,
> They rise, they walk again.

In all of these examples, the animals achieve a kind of symbolic perpetuity which elicits reverence from us. Why do we view them so? Perhaps we sublimate fear of our own mortality by projecting onto kindred spirits some kind of immortality, mediated through art.

Next, and based more directly upon observation than on our own projection of animal freedom, we reverence animals for particular excellences: strength, fleetness, beauty, size, endurance—

whichever qualities are suprahuman. Thus Byron's hero Manfred exclaims to the eagles in the Alps:

> Thou art gone
> where the eye cannot follow thee; but thine
> yet pierces downward, onward or above,
> with a pervading vision. Beautiful!

And today, "The eagle is my power, / And my fan is an eagle," asserts the Native American poet Scott Momaday. In "The Sea-Elephant," William Carlos Williams summons hyperboles—"a kind of heaven," "greatest," "bounty," and "enormous"—to describe that other mammal, hyperboles which diminish us by comparison. Let us recall the grandeur of Neptune's carriage, his wild horses rising from the waters in *The Aeneid*[5]:

> He assured
> And cheered the goddess in this way, then yoked
> His team with gold, fitted the foaming bits
> In their wild mouths, and let the reins run free,
> Flying light on the crests in his blue car.
> Waves calmed and quieted, the long sea-swell
> Smoothed out under his thundering axle-tree,
> And storm clouds thinned away in heaven's vast air.
> Now came the diverse shapes of his companions,
> Enormous whales and Glaucus' hoary troops.

For Philip Larkin it is endurance, not scale, which prompts exclamatory praise in his poem "Livings":

> Mussels, limpets,
> Husband their tenacity
> In the freezing slither—
> Creatures, I cherish you!

Because they possess *some* surpassing power, we can invest animals with the concentrated intensity of the symbol. For Navajo and Pueblo Indians, for Eskimos, for instance, an arrow-headed serpent often depicts lightning; to control the snake is to control the otherwise uncontrollable thunderstorm. Symbols and talismans frequently domesticate fear by giving it a shape that can be incorporated into the mythopoetic imagination. Thus, poems about whales by W. S. Merwin, Mark Strand, Gary Snyder, and James Dickey praise in this mammal a "terrible beauty." By coupling terror to beauty, we can transmute what would have been pure terror into a feeling of sublimity. Paradoxically, human beings find something liberating about the contemplation of scale beyond the human. We require something grander than ourselves from which to infer sublimity. Thus, by extension the horse in its beauty acquires the epithet "noble," becoming God's messenger. In this manner we elevate physical attributes to moral ones. Just so, the modern Greek poet Cavafy pictures the "noble horses" of Achilles, though immortal themselves, "shedding their tears for the never-ending calamity of death . . . indignant and sad that Patroclus was slain."[6] Their nobility of aspect is transmuted into nobility of sentiment.

When we select one attribute as a moral power we wish to appropriate, extending it beyond the merely physical, the animal can also serve as a signpost to a better human life. The seventeenth-century Chinese writer Wang Yen, after relating stories of dogs who had saved their masters' lives, dubs them "saint-teachers." When Spanish bulls are bred for the ring, their breeders select them neither for weight nor ferocity but for a quality they term "nobility," by which they designate a nature that will be true to itself to the end, not failing under pain. In accordance with this type of symbolic or emblematic representation of animals, Saint John was called "the eagle" by the Church evangelists for the soaring power of his thought in the Gospel's prologue. (Conversely, when Plato wished to illustrate the dangers of lust, he likened it to "a Rebel Horse.")

Animals presented this way serve as emblems of a moral life, or at least a moral awakening. Thus, the last stanza and a half of Robert Penn Warren's poem "Original Sin: Part of a Short

Story" moves outward from the description of a dramatic but actual encounter with a large animal at night on the road to prophetical questioning, which the encounter provokes about the larger truth of men's lives:

> We had seen what we
> Had come to see, Nature's beauty,
> But not what in the uncoiling
> Of Time, Time being what it is,
> We would come to see. Now under
> White gaze in high darkness of in-
> different stars, unknowing, word-
> less, we lower swung, lower, past
> Tormented stone of crags; then in
> Black maw of conifer forest.
> And what beast might there wait.
>
> What beast with fang more white, with claw
> More scimitar, with gaze of blaze
> More metaphysical, patient
> As stone in a roar that seems like
> Silence, waiting, waiting, will wait
> Where and however long? — While we,
> By other crags, by moonlit field,
> By what star-tumbling stream, or through
> What soundless snow the wipers groan
> To cope with, on roads poor-mapped, move
> Toward what foetal, fatal truth
> Our hearts unguiltily conceal
> Beneath the pretense of life's jollity.

A strikingly similar epiphany occurs in Elizabeth Bishop's "The Moose" — "A moose has come out of / the impenetrable wood," and the bus from which the animal is sighted stops, while the wondering passengers "exclaim" over her. The bus ride commenced with a description of domestic scenes, houses, and people; the unexpected glimpse of the animal, as in the Warren poem, extends the poem outward to the "grand and otherworldly," and raises an almost unanswerable question:

> Taking her time,
> she looks the bus over,
> grand, otherworldly.
> Why, why do we feel
> (we all feel) this sweet
> sensation of joy?

Animals provoke metaphysical, "otherworldly" questions about our own human life because they are both wild and "other." Poems embodying a reverence toward animals implicate by contrast the dullness and sameness of our own human existence and our yearning to escape the vacuum of individuality that, especially in our time, is characterized by a loss of belief in religious, familial, and other authoritative and cohesive structures which could provide such extension. Our highly individualistic society has burdened us with isolation, alienation, and angst. We have grown far away from intuitive knowledge of ourselves and our world, and therefore from the kind of immediate reflexive action that animals rely upon for their own protection and perpetuation. This is the third quality that elicits a reverential attitude, the one we designate as integrity. Within the context of reverence, integrity signifies particularly the sense of being at home, integrated (integer = whole), in the world. Thus, Gerard Manley Hopkins observes that young lambs bound " . . . as if the earth had flung them, not themselves," whereas Rilke's "First Elegy," by contrast, laments for all humankind, "We are not at home in this interpreted world." Being "at home," animals require no intermediary, no priest. In "Move," Alicia Ostriker envies the turtle, asserting that we humans are "Thirsty for a destiny like this, / An absolute right choice." She envies the certainty of their knowledge, when and how to "move," something she (and we) lack. For human beings, artifice must compensate for the highly developed sensory faculties of other creatures. We use radar "to home"; the tern uses its own inner migratory map.

"Integrity" is the word chosen by Ammons in "Easter Morning" to describe the natural, graceful (grace-filled) flight of the birds, whose motion is the externalization of the religious emotion centered on the resurrection at Easter. As Emerson has written, "Every natural fact / Is a symbol of some spiritual fact." Agreeing, Ammons describes the eagles' flight as "sacred."

Pablo Neruda uses the word "integral" to characterize his "Dream Horses," who, because they are "all of a piece," enable him to transcend human limitations:

> What a morning is here! What a milk-heavy glow
> in the air, integral, all of a piece,
> intending some good! I have heard its red horses
> naked to bridle and iron, shimmering, whinnying
> there.
>
> Mounted, I soar over churches,
> gallop the garrisons empty of soldiers
> while a dissolute army pursues me.
> Eucalyptus, its eyes raze the darkness
> and the bell of its galloping body strikes home.
>
> I need but a spark of that perduring brightness,
> my jubilant kindred to claim that inheritance.

In general, reverence toward animals has been strengthened by changes in our cultural mores—"wildness" is not the pejorative term today that it was for the Victorians ("nature red in tooth and claw," as Tennyson described it). We are beginning to reject the unlimited and arrogant sense of supremacy which late-nineteenth-century empire building and industrialization imparted to many European political powers and their peoples. Rather, "wildness" is a term of approbation today, extending Jean-Jacques Rousseau's notion of "the noble savage" to the animal.

To be "wild" is to be guiltless in more ways than that of sexual appetite. After the Holocaust, after the atomic bombings of Hiroshima and Nagasaki, after Dresden and the massacres at My Lai, a sense of the relativity of guilt has come upon us. To kill in order to eat seems innocence indeed. "No man is guileless as the serpent," asserts Denise Levertov.

So viewed, animals seem to live within a more redeemable world, a world closer to God's grace. And for this, too, we envy them, wonder at them. Reverential poems about animals, focused on their freedom, suprahuman gifts, and integrity, originate in the consciousness of our own transgression, with consequent loss of power and connection. In Berry's poem, "wild" describes creatures untouched by human lives, itself a condition of innocence; conversely, in the opening lines the human being, the poet, comes to them "wild" with despair.

The Peace of Wild Things

WENDELL BERRY

When despair for the world grows in me
and I wake in the night at the least sound
in fear of what my life and my children's lives may be,
I go and lie down where the wood drake
rests in his beauty on the water, and the great heron feeds.
I come into the peace of wild things
who do not tax their lives with forethought
of grief. I come into the presence of still water.
And I feel above me the day-blind stars
waiting with their light. For a time
I rest in the grace of the world, and am free.

The Snake

D. H. LAWRENCE

A snake came to my water-trough
On a hot, hot day, and I in pyjamas for the heat,
To drink there.

In the deep, strange-scented shade of the great dark carob-tree
I came down the steps with my pitcher
And must wait, must stand and wait, for there he was at the
    trough before me.

He reached down from a fissure in the earth-wall in the gloom
And trailed his yellow-brown slackness soft-bellied down,
    over the edge of the stone trough
And rested his throat upon the stone bottom,
And where the water had dripped from the tap, in a small
    clearness,
He sipped with his straight mouth,
Softly drank through his straight gums, into his slack long
    body,
Silently.

Someone was before me at my water-trough,
And I, like a second comer, waiting.

He lifted his head from his drinking, as cattle do,
And looked at me vaguely, as drinking cattle do,
And flickered his two-forked tongue from his lips, and
    mused a moment,
And stooped and drank a little more,
Being earth-brown, earth-golden from the burning bowels of
    the earth
On the day of Sicilian July, with Etna smoking.

The voice of my education said to me
He must be killed,
For in Sicily the black, black snakes are innocent, the gold
    are venomous.

And voices in me said, If you were a man
You would take a stick and break him now, and finish him off.

But must I confess how I liked him,
How glad I was he had come like a guest in quiet, to drink
    at my water-trough
And depart peaceful, pacified, and thankless,
Into the burning bowels of this earth?

Was it cowardice, that I dared not kill him?
Was it perversity, that I longed to talk to him?
Was it humility, to feel so honoured?
I felt so honoured.

And yet those voices:
If you were not afraid, you would kill him!

And truly I was afraid, I was most afraid,
But even so, honoured still more
That he should seek my hospitality
From out the dark door of the secret earth.

He drank enough
And lifted his head, dreamily, as one who has drunken,
And flickered his tongue like a forked night on the air, so black;
Seeming to lick his lips,
And looked around like a god, unseeing, into the air,
And slowly turned his head,
And slowly, very slowly, as if thrice adream,
Proceeded to draw his slow length curving round
And climb again the broken bank of my wall-face.

And as he put his head into that dreadful hole,
And as he slowly drew up, snake-easing his shoulders, and
    entered farther,
A sort of horror, a sort of protest against his withdrawing
    into the horrid black hole,
Deliberately going into the blackness, and slowly drawing
    himself after,
Overcame me now his back was turned.

I looked round, I put down my pitcher,
I picked up a clumsy log
And threw it at the water-trough with a clatter.

I think it did not hit him,
But suddenly that part of him that was left behind convulsed
    in undignified haste,
Writhed like lightning, and was gone
Into the black hole, the earth-lipped fissure in the wall-front,
At which, in the intense still noon, I stared with fascination.

And immediately I regretted it.
I thought how paltry, how vulgar, what a mean act.
I despised myself and the voices of my accursed human
    education.

And I thought of the albatross,
And I wished he would come back, my snake.

For he seemed to me again like a king,
Like a king in exile, uncrowned in the underworld,
Now due to be crowned again.

And so, I missed my chance with one of the lords
Of life.
And I have something to expiate;
A pettiness.

Some Beasts

PABLO NERUDA

It was the twilight of the iguana.
From the rainbow-arch of the battlements,
his long tongue like a lance
sank down in green leaves,
and a swarm of ants, monks with feet chanting, crawled
off into the jungle,
the guanaco, thin as oxygen
in the wide peaks of cloud,
went along wearing his shoes of gold,
while the llama opened his honest eyes
on the breakable neatness
of a world full of dew.
The monkeys braided a sexual
thread that went on and on
along the shores of the dawn,
demolishing walls of pollen
and startling the butterflies of Muzo
into flying violets.
It was the night of the alligators,
the pure night, crawling
with snouts emerging from the ooze,
and out of the sleepy marshes
the confused noise of scaly plates
returned to the ground where they began.

The jaguar brushed the leaves
with a luminous absence,
the puma runs through the branches
like a forest fire,
while the jungle's drunken eyes
burn from inside him.

The badgers scratch the river's
feet, scenting the nest
whose throbbing delicacy
they attack with red teeth.

And deep in the huge waters
the enormous anaconda lies
like the circle around the earth,
covered with ceremonies of mud,
devouring, religious.

translated by James Wright

Easter Morning

A. R. AMMONS

I have a life that did not become,
that turned aside and stopped,
astonished;
I hold it in me like a pregnancy or
as on my lap a child
not to grow or grow old but dwell on

it is to his grave I most
frequently return and return
to ask what is wrong, what was
wrong, to see it all by
the light of a different necessity
but the grave will not heal
and the child,
stirring, must share my grave
with me, an old man having
gotten by on what was left .

when I go back to my home country in these
fresh far-away days, it's convenient to visit
everybody, aunts and uncles, those who used to say,
look how he's shooting up, and the
trinket aunts who always had a little
something in their pocketbooks, cinnamon bark,
or a penny or nickel, and uncles who
were the rumored fathers of cousins
who whispered of them as of great, if
troubled presences, and school
teachers, just about everybody older
(and some younger) collected in one place

waiting, particularly, but not for
the mother and the father there, too, and others
close, close as burrowing
under skin, all in the graveyard
assembled, done for, and the world they
used to wield, have trouble and joy
in, gone

the child in me that could not become
was not ready for others to go,
to go on into change, blessings and
horrors, but stands there by the road
where the mishap occurred, crying out for
help, come and fix this or we
can't get by, but the great ones who
were to return, they could not or did
not hear and went in a flurry and
now, I say in the graveyard, here
lies the flurry, now it can't come
back with help or helpful asides, now
we all buy the bitter
incompletions, pick up the knots of
horror, silently raving, and go on
crashing into empty ends not
completions, not rondures the fullness
has come into and spent itself from
I stand on the stump
of a child, whether myself
or my little brother who died, and
yell as far as I can, I cannot leave this place, for
for me it is the dearest and the worst,
it is life nearest to life which is
life lost: it is my place where
I must stand and fail,
calling attention with tears
to the branches not lofting

boughs into space, to the barren
air that holds the world that was my world

though the incompletions
(and completions) burn out
standing in the flash high-burn
momentary structure of ash, still it
is a picture-book, letter-perfect
Easter morning: I have been for a
walk: the wind is tranquil: the brook
works without flashing in an abundant
tranquility: the birds are lively with
voice: I saw something I had
never seen before: two great birds,
maybe eagles, blackwinged, whitenecked
and -headed, come from the south oaring
the great wings steadily; they went
directly over me, high up, and on
due north: but then one bird,
the one behind, veered a little to the
left and the other bird kept on seeming
not to notice for a minute: the first
began to circle as if looking for something,
        coasting, resting its wings
on the down side of some of the circles:
the other bird came back and they both
circled, looking perhaps for a draft;
they turned a few more times, possibly
rising—at least, clearly resting—
then flew on falling into distance till
they broke across the local bush and
trees: it was a sight of bountiful
majesty and integrity: the having
patterns and routes, breaking
from them to explore other patterns or
better ways to routes, and then the
return: a dance sacred as the sap in

the trees, permanent in its descriptions
as the ripples round the brook's
ripplestones: fresh as this particular
flood or burn breaking across us now
from the sun.

The Sea-Elephant

WILLIAM CARLOS WILLIAMS

Trundled from
the strangeness of the sea—
a kind of
heaven—

Ladies and Gentlemen!
the greatest
sea-monster ever exhibited
alive

the gigantic
sea-elephant! O wallow
of flesh where
are
there fish enough for
that
appetite stupidity
cannot lessen?

Sick
of April's smallness
the little leaves—

Flesh has lief of you
enormous sea—
Speak!
Blouaugh! (feed
me) my
flesh is riven—
fish after fish into his maw
unswallowing

to let them glide down
gulching back
half spittle half
brine

the troubled eyes—torn
from the sea.
(In
a practical voice) They
ought
to put it back where
it came from.

Gape.
Strange head—
told by older sailors—
rising

bearded
to the surface—and
the only
sense out of them

is that woman's
Yes
it's wonderful but they
ought to

put it
back in the sea where
it came from.
Blouaugh?

Swing—ride
walk
on wires—toss balls
stoop and

contort yourselves—
But I
am love. I am
from the sea—

Blouaugh!
there is no crime save
the too-heavy
body

the sea
held playfully—comes
to the surface
the water

boiling
about the head the cows
scattering
fish dripping from

the bounty
of . . . and spring
they say
Spring is icummen in—

The Eighth Elegy

RAINER MARIA RILKE

All other creatures look into the Open
with their whole eyes. But our eyes,
turned inward, are set all around it like snares,
trapping its way out to freedom.
We know what's out there only from the animal's
face; for we take even the youngest child,
turn him around and force him to look
at the past as formation, not that openness
so deep within an animal's face. Free from death,
we only see it; the free animal
always has its destruction behind
and god ahead, and when it moves,
it moves toward eternity like running springs.
      Not for a single day, no, never have we had
that pure space ahead of us, in which flowers
endlessly open. It is always World
and never Nowhere without No:
that pure, unguarded space we breathe,
always know, and never crave. As a child,
one may lose himself in silence and be
shaken out of it. Or one dies and *is* it.
Once near death, one can't see death anymore
and stares out, maybe with the wide eyes of animals.
If the other weren't there blocking the view,
lovers come close to it and are amazed . . .
It opens up behind the other, almost
an oversight . . . but no one gets past
the other, and the world returns again.
Always facing creation, all we see
is the reflection of the free and open

that we've darkened, or some mute animal
raising its calm eyes and seeing through us,
and through us. This is destiny: to be opposites,
always, and nothing else but opposites.

If this sure animal approaching us
from a different direction had our kind
of consciousness, he'd drag us around
in his wake. But to the animal, his being
is infinite, incomprehensible, and blind
to his condition, pure, like his outward gaze.
And where we see the future, he sees
all, himself in all, and whole forever.

And yet the weight and care of one great sadness
lies on this warm and watching creature.
Because what often overwhelms us
also clings to him—the memory
that what we so strive for now may have been
nearer, truer, and its attachment to us
infinitely tender, once. Here all is distance,
there it was breath. After that first home,
the second seems drafty and a hybrid.
        Oh, blessed are the tiny creatures
who stay in the womb that bore them forever;
oh the joy of the gnat that can still leap *within,*
even on its wedding day; for the womb is all!
And look at the half-certainty of the bird
almost aware of both from birth,
like one of the Etruscan souls rising
from the dead man enclosed inside the space
for which his reclining figure forms a lid.
And how confused is anything that comes
from a womb and has to fly. As if afraid
of itself, it darts through the air
like a crack through a cup, the way a wing
of a bat crazes the porcelain of night.

And we: spectators, always, everywhere,
looking at everything and never *from!*
It floods us. We arrange it. It decays.
We arrange it again, and we decay.

Who's turned us around like this,
so that whatever we do, we always have
the look of someone going away? Just as a man
on the last hill showing him his whole valley
one last time, turns, and stops, and lingers—
so we live, and are forever leaving.

translated by A. Poulin, Jr.

Swan Song

GERALD STERN

A bunch of old snakeheads down by the pond
carrying on the swan tradition—hissing
inside their white bodies, raising and lowering their heads
like ostriches, regretting only the sad ritual
that forced them to waddle back into the water
after their life under the rocks, wishing they could lie again
    in the sun

and dream of spreading their terrifying wings;
wishing, this time, they could sail through the sky like
    horses,
their tails rigid, their white manes fluttering,
their mouths open, their sharp teeth flashing,
drops of mercy pouring from their eyes,
bolts of wisdom from their foreheads.

Beasts

RICHARD WILBUR

Beasts in their major freedom
Slumber in peace tonight. The gull on his ledge
Dreams in the guts of himself the moon-plucked waves below,
And the sunfish leans on a stone, slept
By the lyric water;

In which the spotless feet
Of deer make dulcet splashes, and to which
The ripped mouse, safe in the owl's talon, cries
Concordance. Here there is no such harm
And no such darkness

And the selfsame moon observes
Where, in the warped glass, it sponsors now
The werewolf's painful change. Turning his head away
On the sweaty bolter, he tries to remember
The mood of manhood,

But lies at last, as always,
Letting it happen, the fierce soft fur soft to his face,
Hearing with sharper ears the wind's exciting minors,
The leaves' panic, and the degradation
Of the heavy streams.

Meantime, at high windows
Far from thicket and pad-fall, suitors of excellence
Sigh and turn from their work to construe again the painful
Beauty of heaven, the lucid moon
And the risen hunter,

Making such dreams for me
As told will break their hearts as always, bringing
Monsters into the city, crows on the public statues,
Navies fed to the fish in the dark
Unbridled waters.

The Emu and the Nobilities of Interest

LES A. MURRAY

Weathered blond as a grass tree, a huge Beatles haircut
raises an alert periscope and stares out
over scrub. Her large olivine eggs click
oilily together; her lips of noble plastic
clamped in their expression, her head-fluff a stripe
worn Mohawk style, she bubbles her pale-blue windpipe—
the emu, Dromaius novaehollandiae,
whose stand-in on most continents is an antelope,
looks us in both eyes with her one eye
and her other eye, dignified courageous hump,
feather-swaying condensed camel, Swift Courser of New
    Holland.

Knees backward in toothed three-way boots, you stand,
Dinewan, proud emu, common as the dust
in your sleeveless cloak, returning our interest.
Your shield of fashion's wobbly: you're Quaint, you're
    Native,
even somewhat Bygone. You may be let live
but beware: the blank zones of Serious disdain
are often carte blanche to the darkly human.
Europe's boats on their first strange shore looked humble
but, Mass over, men started renaming the creatures.
Worship turned to interest and had new features.
Now only life survives, if it's made remarkable.

Heraldic bird, our protection is a fable
made of space and neglect. We're remarkable and not;
we're the ordinary discovered on a strange planet.

Are you Early or Late, in the history of birds,
which doesn't exist and is deeply ancient?

My kinships, too, are immemorial and recent,
like my country, which abstracts yours in words.
This distillate of mountains is finely branched, this plain
expanse of dour delicate lives, where the rain,
shrouded slab on the west horizon, is a corrugated revenant
settling its long clay-tipped plumage in a hatching descent.

Rubberneck, stepped sister, I see your eye on our jeep's load.
I think your story is, when you were offered
the hand of evolution you gulped it. Forefinger and thumb
project from your face, but the weighing palm is inside you
collecting the bottletops, nails, wet cement that you famous-
    ly swallow—
your passing muffled show, your serially private museum.
Some truths are now called trivial, though. Only God ap-
    proves them.
Some humans who disdain them make a kind of weather
which, when it grows overt and widespread, we call war.
There we make death trivial and awesome, by rapid turns
    about,
we conscript it to bless us, force-feed it to squeeze the drama out;
indeed we imprison and torture death—this part is called
    peace;
we offer it murder like mendicants, begging for significance.
You rustle dreams of pardon, not fleeing in your hovercraft
    style,
not gliding fast with zinc-flaked legs dangling, feet making
    high-tensile
seesawing impacts. Wasteland parent, barely edible dignitary,
the disinterested spotlight of the lords of interest
and gowned nobles of ennui is a torch of vivid arrest
and blinding after-darkness. But you hint it's a brigand
    sovereignty

after the steady extents of God's common immortality
whose image is daylight detail, aggregate, in process yet
    plumb
to the everywhere focus of one devoid of boredom.

Come into Animal Presence

DENISE LEVERTOV

Come into animal presence.
No man is so guileless as
the serpent. The lonely white rabbit
on the roof is a star
twitching its ears at the rain.
The llama intricately
folding its hind legs to be seated
not disdains but mildly
disregards human approval.
What joy when the insouciant
armadillo glances at us and doesn't
quicken his trotting
across the track into the palm brush.

What is this joy? That no animal
falters, but knows what it must do?
That the snake has no blemish,
that the rabbit inspects his strange surroundings
in white-star silence? The llama
rests in dignity, the armadillo
has some intention to pursue the palm-forest.
Those who were sacred have remained so,
holiness does not dissolve, it is a presence
of bronze, only the sight that saw it
faltered and turned from it.
An old joy returns in holy presence.

With Trumpets and Zithers*

CZESLAW MILOSZ

The dream shared at night by all people has inhabitants,
    hairy animals.
It is a huge and snug forest and everyone entering it walks
    on all fours till dawn through the very thick of the tangle.
Through the wilderness inaccessible to metal objects,
    all-embracing like a warm and deep river.
In satin tunnels the touch distinguishes apples and their color
    that does not recall anything real.
All are quadrupeds, their thighs rejoice at the badger-bear
    softness, their rosy tongues lick the fur of each other.
The "I" is felt with amazement in the heartbeat, but so
    large it cannot be filled by the whole Earth with her
    seasons.
Nor would the skin guarding a different essence trace any
    boundary.
Later on, in crude light, separated into you and me, they try
    with a bare foot pebbles of the floor.
The two-legged, some to the left, some to the right, put on
    their belts, garter, slacks and sandals.
After they move on their stilts, longing after a forest home,
    after low tunnels, after an assigned return to It.

*10

A Name for All

HART CRANE

Moonmoth and grasshopper that flee our page
And still wing on, untarnished of the name
We pinion to your bodies to assuage
Our envy of your freedom—we must maim

Because we are usurpers, and chagrined—
And take the wing and scar it on the hand.
Names we have, even, to clap on the wind;
But we must die, as you, to understand.

I dreamed that all men dropped their names, and sang
As only they can praise, who build their days
With fin and hoof, with wing and sweetened fang
Stuck free and holy in one Name always.

The Horses of Achilles

CAVAFY

When they saw that Patroclus was slain,
who had been so stalwart, and strong, and young,
the horses of Achilles started to weep;
their immortal nature was indignant
at the sight of this work of death.
They would shake their heads and toss their manes,
stamp the ground with their feet, and mourn
Patroclus who they realized was lifeless—undone—
worthless flesh now—his spirit lost—
defenseless—without breath—
returned from life to the great Nothing.

Zeus saw the tears of the immortal horses
and grew sad. "At the wedding of Peleus,"
he said, "I should not have acted so thoughtlessly;
it would have been better my hapless horses
if we had not given you! What are you doing down there,
among woebegone humanity, the plaything of fate?
You for whom neither death nor old age lie in wait,
you are harassed by transitory calamities.
Men have implicated you in their troubles." Yet the two
noble animals went on shedding their tears
for the never-ending calamity of death.

translated by Rae Dalven

Saaka Crested Cranes

DAVID RUBADIRI

The Prison Farm at Saaka
cradles craggy trucks
old and grey
on which pelicans perch;

Saaka they say
is a crater lake,
bottomless—
ringed with banana homes
the feminine complexity
of prison and fertility;

It was in this water of life
as the children call it
that one evening
quiet and still
swooped a troop of crested cranes
Ngaali on the wing,

as we held hands,
swirling upwards
crested high
majestically borne
like priest of Osiris
to nest.

DOMINION

Needlework Picture,
Mary Upelbe, Massachusetts, 1767.

Let us make man in our own image, after our likeness;
and let them have dominion over fish of the sea, and
over fowl of the air, and over the cattle . . . and over
every creeping thing.

GENESIS 1:26

Thou madest him to have dominion over the works of
thy hands; thou hast put all things under his feet. The
fowl of the air, and the fish of the sea, and whatsoever
passeth through the path of the seas.

PSALM 8:6,8

These resonant Biblical passages are probably the first mandate
Westerners think of when we reflect on the relationship of dominion, though of course it goes back much further in history than
the Bible. The Hellenic tradition is summed up in Aristotle's pro-
nouncement that we share senses and appetite with animals, but
humankind alone possesses reason, sufficient grounds to establish
our superiority. The Judeo-Christian tradition, which has most
influenced thinking about sovereignty in the Western world, con-
curs with Aristotle on this question. There exists, they posit, a
scale of ascendancy, with man "naturally" set above the animals.

51

The most significant symbolic action in this schema is that of Adam naming the animals (Genesis 2:19–20):

> And out of the ground the Lord God formed every beast of the field, and every fowl of the air; and brought them unto Adam to see what he would call them: and whatsoever Adam called every living creature, that was the name thereof.
>
> And Adam gave names to all cattle, and to the fowl of the air, and to every beast of the field.

By means of this act, one of the most potent functions of dominion, Adam participates in the godlike function of creativity; the animals are what they are because he has named them. Man gains mastery by virtue of this power since animals come when he calls them. He literally calls them into being. (The Australian aborigines divide their territories by "songlines" inherited from ancestors who sang out "the name of everything that crossed their paths — birds, animals, rocks, waterholes — and so singing the world into existence," as Bruce Chatwin explains in *The Songlines*.[1]) In the Western world, we construe this power as one surety that man is created in the image of God, the Creator. Naming *is* a creative power; "Saying is inventing," Samuel Beckett's character Molloy comments. And Rilke suggests in the "Ninth Duino Elegy":

> Are we, perhaps, here just for saying: House,
> Bridge, Fountain, Gate, Jug, Fruit tree, Window —
> possibly, Pillar, Tower? . . . but for saying,
> remember, oh, for such saying as never the things
> themselves hoped intensely to be.

The compelling quality of this myth of name/identity bestowal is shown by its consistent grip upon the imagination; it is one of those stories, closely linked to the myth of Orpheus, which is retold in every generation. The legend of Orpheus quietening the animals with his lyre, using the voice of his instrument that is really an extension of "saying" or "naming," remains an inexhaustible resource for poets because it dramatizes the magical powers creativity confers on human beings. Art tames ("subdues" is the biblical word) nature; "Music hath charms to soothe the savage breast." Thus we not only bring things into being, but may contour them with our art, or imagination, as Auguste Comte proposed.

The most powerful visualization of dominion is Edward Hicks's series of paintings on the subject of *The Peaceable Kingdom,* that utopian vision in which pacific and fraternal animals are tended by uncorrupted humans. Indeed, the Edenic myth is based on the assumption that there were no *wild,* that is, malevolent, animals in the Garden; humans, in naming them, succeeded in taming them. In 1981 the poet Daniel Hoffman seized upon this theme (as had Marianne Moore and Jon Silkin before him), creating a book-length poem, *Brotherly Love.* Hoffman's book reminds his readers of the double character of dominion: the practical and the spiritual, using animals for human benefit, but at the same time regarding them as a trust. Creation is interpreted as the visible design of God's plan and plenitude of which we are caretakers, not owners. The wellspring for Hicks's vision and Hoffman's poem is the famous passage from Isaiah, that ideal of peaceful coexistence which begins "The lion shall lie down with the lamb." The concluding verse is much less familiar, but contains the important injunction to humankind:

Thou shall not hurt nor destroy
In all my holy mountain:
For the earth shall be full of the knowledge of the Lord,
As the waters cover the sea.

Harmony in creation is present because God's design of order, proceeding from the valuation of all life, confers peace and dignity. The relation of dominion is our human, more limited, expression of an ideal design.

For peoples without advanced and extensive technology, the relationship of dominion continues more intact and is therefore easier to observe; their songs, prayers, and poems ceremonially acknowledge a relationship with the animal upon which human survival depends—for food, clothing, transport, agricultural labor; wealth is counted in animal stock, and success by skill in the hunt. However, in African, Native American, or Eskimo poetry, the practical and the spiritual coexist, the reality of the first making the second unselfconscious and unsentimental. In fact, it is through practical necessities in the relationship between man and beast that the spiritual links remain secured. These people have not needed to summon up from the past neglected memories. Whereas poetry from industrialized societies seems suspect when it introduces notions of anthropomorphism, for example (as we will see in the next section), the intimacy with nature that still characterizes the hunting cultures makes it seemly for them to retain this otherwise artificial device. "My breast-meat and my entrails / I make tasty for eating with luscious blubber," runs the contemporary "Song of the Ptarmigan" by the Eskimo poet Niaqunuaq. When a human life is pitted against an animal's, as it still is in some of these cultures, that creature's importance dominates the human life. He is an adversary worth understanding well. For the contemporary reader who cannot visualize, except as a postnuclear apocalyptic void, a *War of the Worlds* such as H. G. Wells predicted, imagining the actual threat in which our ancestors lived in hunting societies, the danger of a known adversary, accomplishes something creative. Indeed, hand-to-hand contests between Eskimo and polar bear are often recounted within the Eskimo culture as moments of "awe and apotheosis," Barry Lopez reports in *Arctic Dreams*.

Even in cities, there was a closer interdependence between people and animals in past times. In the Middle Ages, for example, Spanish and Moorish cities protected kites, ravens, and even vultures because these scavenging birds performed a needed and valued service, cleaning the cities of their waste. But in much of the Western world, machinery, now the indispensable tool, is tended with the care previously bestowed upon animals. Moreover, today's industrial development, which evicts animals from their natural grounds in such formerly uninhabited areas as the jungle and the tundra, is more of a threat to species survival than hunting itself.

The arrogance and blindness with which we have for centuries discharged our stewardship toward the earth and other living beings are finally a matter of common concern. Our fear for the future existence of *our* planet, as we call it, is challenging many inherited abuses of dominion. We are made aware, both through our own experience and by the media, that air, earth, and water, elements necessary to sustain life, are no longer present in limitless amounts, nor are our remaining resources pure. Acid rain has already felled major forests. Rivers and lakes have been destroyed by industrial waste, so that fish can no longer survive in them. The ecological system of the jungle is ruptured to build landing fields, and, as a consequence, some bird species disappear forever. Oil spills kill ocean life for miles around. The ecosystem we have taken for granted is being destroyed — not by glaciers, fires, or animal contest — but by us, and at a rate far exceeding anything we can reverse. Books such as Jonathan Schell's *The Fate of the Earth*[2] and films like *The Emerald Forest,* about the destruction of rain forest and Indian peoples in Brazil, strike a responsive chord in our individual awareness, as their popularity attests. Organizations such as The World Wildlife Fund, Greenpeace, and the Animal Liberation Front have developed to safeguard animal rights and to determine the extent of our ethical obligations toward other creatures.

Why *should* we care if species die out? Why can't we live without whales? After all, we live without dinosaurs and hairy mammoths. Is it that we value these species for their rarity, as the commercial value of any commodity increases with rarity? Certainly that commercial value prevails for the furs and the ivory tusks we trade and sell. Is it that those species now dying out are, unlike the dinosaurs and hairy mammoths, our contemporaries on the planet? Concern for species survival may stem in part from the guilty admission that we are accelerating the rate of species extinction. Thus, in "An Awful Moment," poet X. J. Kennedy rebukes the conspicuous consumption which provides one significant motive for animal slaughter: "Why does one skinny neck need a whole furry fox?" But there is a more subtle, even atavistic reason why we care. The fact that many species have become extinct within the span of one generation makes it easy for us to project the time when we, too, will be an endangered species.

The extent to which our attitude toward animals has changed from a justification of predation is manifest in many poems that see our treatment of animals as a microcosm of what we do to ourselves, caging and enslaving each other, forgetful of Blake's admonition that "A robin redbreast in a cage / Puts all heaven in a rage." On the caged animal, here is Adrienne Rich, for instance, in "The Lioness":

> I see what she is seeing:
> between her and the river's flood,
> the volcano veiled in rainbow,
> a pen that measures three yards square.
> Lashed bars.
> The cage.
> The penance.

Similarly, although the title of the novel by Maya Angelou *I Know Why the Caged Bird Sings* is a metaphor for the black experience in America, the entrapment of urban life enables most of us to empathize.

In Philip Booth's "Creatures," the poet, viewing the unicorn tapestries, reflects how "this late in the world / we have come to hunt ourselves":

> And his wounds—
> > that one of our kind, not for once
> but for all, should so attack him—
> > how the small blood
> drips from his side, how
> > carefully he lies in the
> > flowers
> we know still: iris and
> > daisies, columbines, bluets,
> and red and gold blooms
> > beyond number or name. How can
> > it be

```
                      this late in the world
                                          we have also come to hunt
                                          ourselves,
           ourselves in this creature,
                                          to hunt him in us.
```

For the human race, one of the widespread traumas of the twentieth century, political exile, duplicates the experience of the
hunt, and Russian poet Marina Tsvetayeva selects from animal
imagery the most telling analogy for her own "Homesickness"
in exile:

> It's all the same to me, captive
> lion what faces I move through
> bristling, or what human crowd will
> cast me out as it must
>
> into myself, into my separate internal
> world, a Kamchatka bear without ice.
> *translated by Elaine Feinstein*

In fact, the responsibilities of dominion necessitate coping with
new scientific possibilities, and with their implications for us as
well as for animals. A newspaper article (*Boston Globe,* May 3,
1987) reporting that genetic engineers may be able to "patent"
new forms of animal life, also records the horror with which the
news of this scientific advance was met. James Fox, scientific director of the Humane Society of the United States, declared: "Not
only are these genetic engineers playing God. They are assum-
ing dominion over God." The general public, too, perceives such
control as hubris; the selection of who will live and who will not,
previously left to nature and God, mysteries beyond our fathom-
ing, may now be controlled by the likes of us through biotech-
nology. The hue and cry raised at the prospect of "patenting"
animals reflects not only our mistrust of technology and its prom-
ised "progress," but also the depth of our human identification
with animals. The unstated but powerful fear is that but a short
step further we will have created the monster that will control

us. It is the nightmare of Frankenstein becoming an actuality.

If "naming" is a power of dominion which elevates man to near divinity through the exercise of a creative power, we must also reckon with our near-divine capacity for destruction. Auden, in his poem "The Sabbath," characterizes *Homo sapiens* as "bloody-minded," killing for enjoyment. The animals, to the contrary, appear innocent in their bloodshedding. Wryly, Auden subverts the gratification we derive from our godlike power of destruction—though we are the animals' betters, he writes, we are "Their Lonely Betters." Under this double burden of destructiveness and loneliness who can any longer enthuse with Renaissance Hamlet, "What a piece of work is man! how noble in reason! how infinite in faculty! . . . in action how like an angel! In apprehension how like a god! . . . the paragon of animals!" Rather, poems like Auden's stress that our advantage lies not in the moral or rational superiority upon which Hamlet muses, but in *force*. This consciousness is part of a modern interpretation of dominion, overturning the earlier belief in inevitable progress, which justified our rule over the rest of creation. This view pointed to the fact that the creation of man on the sixth day was the culmination of creation (though the animals were created on the same day), before God rested on the seventh—as if all other species were but rehearsals for us.

It would be sentimental and fallacious to think that human rapacity toward animals has arisen recently. Humankind has been slaughtering animals since prehistory, for hides, bone, blubber, meat. For bait when trapping and fishing. For food while out on the hunt. This is true for native populations—Eskimos, Maoris, Polynesians, Native Americans—who have indeed contributed to extinction of species. What is different is that the basic philosophies of these peoples accord with an ethical attitude toward animal life which we in the Western world are just beginning to formulate. In this view of hunting, for example, the idea of the "gift" predominates over the hunt itself. Eskimos propitiate with gifts the polar bears they kill. The Nemadi believe the soul of the dead beast resides in its bones and take care to bury them in case the dogs defile them, relates Bruce Chatwin in *The Songlines*.

The spirit of our own age, even in developed countries, seeks a reinterpretation of dominion in more responsible terms. Whereas in the eighteenth and nineteenth centuries gifts of wild or exotic animals were commonly presented to the nobility and crowned heads of Europe by the explorers whose expeditions they had patronized, now data are being gathered in the field by anthropologists and marine biologists, by naturalists and many other scientists in order to perpetuate species by understanding their requirements.[3] For the average person the delights of whale and seal watches or safaris whose goal is observation rather than blood sport substitute a respect for animals which is not possessive, which does not reduce other forms of life to trophies. This respect is an important step in the transformation of our attitude.

The conception of "the other," which too easily slopes off into "the suspect," and from there to "the enemy," can only flourish in the absence of knowledge and exchange between creatures, as between the sexes and among nations. We must develop a concept of "other" that merely signifies "apart from" before we can approach animals with the right questions—what are their spatial conceptions, so clearly different from ours? how does their different temporal sense control migratory patterns? what in their behavior is attributable to individuation within the species? and so on. These are questions that may eventually be answered by scientific observation and research, but an imaginative leap must pose them first. Though in the relation of fraternity we will look closely at how animals function as a metaphor for us, that is, for the human condition, we should never forget that they have an existence apart from ours. But an effort to envision the world before or without human beings is an unusual enterprise for the average person, because our habits of thinking are so anthropocentric, empowered as we are by our weapons, tools, and agricultural know-how, which we have used, in many cases, to evict or eliminate animals. If we fail in this attempt, if we reduce dominion to a utilitarian value-system, we are stranded in a narrow and uneasy relation to them, crowding out other imaginative relations literature demonstrates we are eager to retain. In Mark Strand's poem "Shooting Whales," the drama of the day's fearful whale hunt finishes with the poet in bed at night, feeling the whales "luring [him] . . . into the murmurous waters of sleep." The poem ends, then, not with images of violence, but with an ongoing connection the imagination insists upon.

We see this same need to fabricate a larger connection when we try to account for the remarkable success of James Herriot's anecdotal accounts of his veterinarian practice in Yorkshire, England. The popularity of Herriot's books, expanded to television now, attests to our desire for a dominion which could confer a more organic existence upon us, one rooted in a wide community, respectful of animals and fitting into the natural world. Living, as so many people do, on anonymous streets in faceless cities, living at best in nuclear families, moving frequently, with few inherited attachments to place or kin, we harbor an unsatisfied longing for the pastoral ties and strong sense of place that Herriot's life, this kind of dominion, seems to offer. Perhaps erroneously, we see a life such as his, despite its physical hardships, as much simpler—less ratiocinative, closer to instinct and nurture. We sense deeper and broader attachments, fewer changes; this is one of its strongest appeals.

In much the same spirit, but deriving from a different culture, contemporary poet Gary Snyder in "Mother Earth: Her Whales" adopts as a model the cultural pattern of Native Americans— their relation to the earth, to polytheistic nature gods, to animals—in his effort to fashion an alternative mode of respect and connection within the relation of dominion.

And, in addition to the Native American cultures, we possess many other cultural precedents for such an attitude toward dominion, if we wish to use this relation as a touchstone of our own humanity. The Psalmist of the Bible employs the shepherd caring for his flock as the central metaphor of dominion: "The Lord is my shepherd." If Christ is the lamb of God, we, too, are His sheep who "shall safely graze." Much in English literary tradition—Milton's *Lycidas,* Bunyan's *Pilgrim's Progress,* Blake's *Songs of Innocence*—enlarges upon this metaphor. We are to stand in the same relation to the animal world as God does toward us— though we are His sheep, we are their shepherds.

A speckled cat and a tame hare
Eat at my hearthstone
And sleep there;
And both look up to me alone
For learning and defence
As I look up to Providence.

"TWO SONGS OF A FOOL"

W. B. YEATS

Nor is this spiritual dimension of caretaking unrewarded:

The wild deer, wandering here and there,
Keeps the human soul from care.

FROM *AUGURIES OF INNOCENCE*

WILLIAM BLAKE

The Lioness

ADRIENNE RICH

The scent of her beauty draws me to her place.
The desert stretches, edge from edge.
Rock. Silver grasses. Drinking-hole.
The starry sky.
The lioness pauses
in her back-and-forth pacing of three yards square
and looks at me. Her eyes
are truthful. They mirror rivers,
seacoasts, volcanoes, the warmth
of moon-bathed promontories.
Under her haunches' golden hide
flows an innate, half-abnegated power.
Her walk
is bounded. Three square yards
encompass where she goes.

In country like this, I say, the problem is always
one of straying too far, not of staying
within bounds. There are caves,
high rocks, you don't explore. Yet you know
they exist. Her proud, vulnerable head
sniffs toward them. It is her country, she
knows they exist.

I come towards her in the starlight.
I look into her eyes
as one who loves can look,
entering the space behind her eyeballs,
leaving myself outside.
So, at last, through her pupils,

I see what she is seeing:
between her and the river's flood,
the volcano veiled in rainbow,
a pen that measures three yards square.
Lashed bars.
The cage.
The penance.

Adam's Task

Thou, paw-paw-paw; thou, glurd; thou, spotted
    Glurd; thou, whitestap, lurching through
The high-grown brush; thou, plaint-footed,
    Implex; thou, awagabu.

Every burrower, each flier
    Came for the name he had to give:
Gay, first work, ever to be prior,
    Not yet sunk to primitive.

Thou, verdle; thou, McFleery's pomma;
    Thou; thou; thou—three types of grawl;
Thou, flisket; thou, kabasch; thou, comma-
    Eared mashawk; thou, all; thou, all.

Were, in a fire of becoming,
    Laboring to be burned away,
Then work, half-measuring, half-humming,
    Would be as serious as play.

Thou, pambler; thou, rivarn; thou, greater
    Wherret, and thou, lesser one;
Thou, sproal; thou, zant; thou, lily-eater.
    Naming's over. Day is done.

To *the* Maker of *"A Peaceable Kingdom"**

DANIEL HOFFMAN

You, or thee, as thou preferred to be addressed,
were never free of the again: the sleek
musculature of tawny long-tailed jungle cats
uncoiling in the foreground of your mind, wolf and
lambkin, bear and stolid ox as well, but why in
that block-jawed portrait by your cousin Tom (who
won what fame is his with a beardless image of
young Abe before he freed the slaves) does the
square-muzzled lion in his painting of you at your
painting look so much like you? So writhed the
menagerie of your mind, wrestling with that Great
Schism among the Friends—

> whether the Soul is saved
> by inwardly
> pursuing virtue
>
> withdrawing from
> the world because
> the world rejects
>
> the Seed of Light—
> How can Quaker
> ploughshares tax the soil
>
> to pay for guns, for troops
> to set the torch
> to Indian villages?

*Edward Hicks

The Friends step down
from the Assembly, so
to harrow
individual
virtue, from
the world apart.

They read their Bibles
by their guttering
light, until

they have got
the Parables
by heart or rote.

—Or should they seek the Light
    within the soul
kindled, rekindled from
    that sacred coal
of God's Altar that George Fox
    and William Penn
and the Quaker martyrs
    centuries ago
were warmed by, as your cousin
    Elias,
Whitman's father's friend
    on Long Island preached,
and in whose stead
    you testified
in Pennsylvania with
    recriminations
on First days of men
    as good and firm
in their belief
    as thee in thine?

—Wrenched with sorrow, it is then thy mind dwells
upon the Child, in infant frock disposed among the
creatures as in Richard Westall's illustration in

the Bible: the gift of circumstance to the need
your art—that of a copyist, you thought—required.
Your gift was what you made of what you copied: it
was you or thee, as thee would rather, alone who
traced Penn's Treaty with the Indians beside the
Christ Child to say that peace is possible in thy
own soul with his ship the Welcome on the homely
Delaware behind the Shackamaxon Elm. See, placid
ripples glimmer beneath the mountains of the Water
Gap with Child, leopard, fatlings, lions, calves
disporting on a foreground mound. Sixty times that
we know of you laboriously made—all its details
different in each rendering—this dream your
patient hand enacted into forms, shapes, colors, a
frieze that still your mind sees all afresh as
though the scene had never yet been painted, and
must be. Here, one time among those many, every
figure found the place in the design you didn't
know was that which best fulfilled its purpose, the
place your hand was seeking: the Child's hand
holding the Branch of Jesse, which is the vine,
extending like Penn's hand, his to the sachems but
the Child's poised with the Branch from which the
Blood of Jesse flows in the sky above the vessel,
while on shore tame and savage creatures of this
world balance each other in imperfect symmetry of
twinned fulfillments, Heavenly figure close at hand
and large, the mortals very small and far away.
The land is wilderness gentled to pastoral without
a dwelling, house or barn intruding upon the
pureness of its possibility.

This, beneath a mild, inviting sky you have
bequeathed us. It was well no patron sent you from
your craftsman's shop in Newtown with your
paintpots of flat colors to the Royal Academy for
pagan tutelage; left among your simple people with
your gifts, your deep self-doubts and your one
Book, you've given us this scene, framed between
the couplets you made rhymes of from Isaiah's

verses, filling the corners with square medallions
of the Dove descending between the words "Meekness"
"Innocence" "Liberty"—spoken by the ancients and
ourselves in tongues:

> The phrases heard are praises
> of the Lord and Manito
>
> before the Spirit
> withdrew and the Light clouded—
>
> O could our life be blessed
> as it seemed to the Founder!
>
> What though his bequest, his quest
> quicken, then founder;
>
> what though our history lunge
> against Time's prison,
>
> in the lovely simplicity
> of your intricate icon
>
> we see how the soul, though bound
> in the body's cell
>
> uses nerves, bones, brain,
> musculature of the living
>
> man in strife
> with his imperfections
>
> till from woe, from pain
> —yours—many come
>
> a completed image,
> a Peaceable Kingdom

of Brotherly Love, as Penn
from his own sufferings

conceived, from his own being
convinced that the Light

as that of God shines now
as ever it shone

in this commonwealth
of our birth

where the first red breath
the child draws

howls, because necessity
necessity

thrusts us down
to earth, to earth.

Never Again Would Birds' Song Be the Same

ROBERT FROST

He would declare and could himself believe
That the birds there in all the garden round
From having heard the daylong voice of Eve
Had added to their own an oversound,
Her tone of meaning but without the words.
Admittedly an eloquence so soft
Could only have had an influence on birds
When call or laughter carried it aloft.
Be that as may be, she was in their song.
Moreover her voice upon their voices crossed
Had now persisted in the woods so long
That probably it never would be lost.
Never again would birds' song be the same.
And to do that to birds was why she came.

Mother Earth: Her Whales

GARY SNYDER

An owl winks in the shadows
A lizard lifts on tiptoe, breathing hard
Young male sparrow stretches up his neck,
        big head, watching—

The grasses are working in the sun. Turn it green.
Turn it sweet. That we may eat.
Grow our meat.

Brazil says "sovereign use of Natural Resources"
Thirty thousand kinds of unknown plants.
The living actual people of the jungle
        sold and tortured—
And a robot in a suit who peddles a delusion called "Brazil"
        can speak for *them?*

        The whales turn and glisten, plunge
                and sound and rise again,
        Hanging over subtly darkening deeps
        Flowing like breathing planets
                in the sparkling whorls of
                        living light—

And Japan quibbles for words on
        what kinds of whales they can kill?
A once-great Buddhist nation
        dribbles methyl mercury
        like gonorrhea
                in the sea.

Père David's Deer, the Elaphure,
Lived in the tule marshes of the Yellow River

Two thousand years ago—and lost its home to rice—
The forests of Lo-yang were logged and all the silt &
Sand flowed down, and gone, by 1200 A.D.—

Wild Geese hatched out in Siberia
                head south over basins of the Yang, the Huang,
                what we call "China"
On flyways they have used a million years.
Ah China, where are the tigers, the wild boars,
                the monkeys,
                        like the snows of yesteryear
Gone in a mist, a flash, and the dry hard ground
Is parking space for fifty thousand trucks.
IS man most precious of all things?
—then let us love him, and his brothers, all those
Fading living beings—

North America, Turtle Island, taken by invaders
                who wage war around the world.
May ants, may abalone, otters, wolves and elk
Rise! and pull away their giving
                from the robot nations.

Solidarity. The People.
Standing Tree People!
Flying Bird People!
Swimming Sea People!
Four-legged, two-legged, people!

How can the head-heavy power-hungry politic scientist
Government   two-world   Capitalist-Imperialist
Third-world   Communist   paper-shuffling male
                non-farmer   jet-set   bureaucrats
Speak for the green of the leaf? Speak for the soil?

(Ah Margaret Mead . . . do you sometimes dream of
        Samoa?)

The robots argue how to parcel out our Mother Earth
To last a little longer
                like vultures flapping
Belching, gurgling,
                near a dying Doe.

"In yonder field a slain knight lies—
We'll fly to him and eat his eyes
                with a down
        derry derry derry down down."

                An Owl winks in the shadow
                A lizard lifts on tiptoe
                        breathing hard
                The whales turn and glisten
                        plunge and
Sound, and rise again
Flowing like breathing planets

In the sparkling whorls

Of living light.

Hymn to the Spirit of the Air

IGPAKUHAK

i stand here humbly
with extended arms,
for the spirit of the air
has brought down game for me!

i stand here   .
surrounded by great joy,
for a reindeer with tall antlers
carelessly exposed his flanks to me!

ah, how i crouched
in my hunter's hide!
but scarcely had i glimpsed his flanks,
than my arrow pierced them,
haunch to haunch.

and then, beloved reindeer,
as you pissed there,
as you fell,
i was surrounded by great joy!

o stand here humbly
with extended arms,
for the spirit of the air
has brought down game for me!

i stand here humbly
with extended arms,
surrounded by great joy:
an old bull-seal
was blowing through his breathing-hole,

and i, a little man,
stood upright over him.
the tension
made my body longer,
till i drove my harpoon down,
and tied him
to the harpoon-rope.

translated by Tom Lowenstein

Giant Panda

KABIRU ABDU KILA

My folklore has it that you were confined to poles,
That even your dung was ice; apes your ancestors
I was convinced.
But today when you acclimatized in my reserve,
Wore a face the shape of Pythagorean circle,
Crescented limbs, even Darwin's biology is not certain.
You acclimatized in my reserve, thrived on all the
Bamboo I grew, dropped your icy dung.
Judah's Lion's roars no longer match yours,
You are already an eighth wonder,
You are beautiful — which I envy: only Byzantine
Logothethes say you are grotesque.
But despite conservationist's appeal to grow more
Bamboo for your survival, your extinction is imminent.
You will have no fossil record.

Zoo Gardens Revisited

A. K. RAMANUJAN

Once flamingoes reminded me of long-legged aunts in white
cottons, and black-faced monkeys of grave lowbrow uncles
    with
moveable scalps and wrinkled long black hands. Now
    animals remind
me only of animals,

                    orangutans only of orangutans, and of
tuberculosis in the Delhi Zoo. And the symmetric giraffe in
London that split in two trying to mount a coy female who
   gave
him no quarter.

Visitors no longer gape at ostriches, so they tell me, but
shrewdly set their tail feathers on fire with lighter fluid and
cigarette lighters. So ostriches in zoos no longer hide their
heads in sand as they do in proverbs.

Some, they say, feed bananas to the dying race of ring-tailed
monkeys, bananas with small exquisite needles in them. So
    monkeys
in zoos no longer eat bananas as they still do in temple cities
and Jungle Books.

Tigresses, I hear, go barren, or superintended by curious
officials adulterate their line with half-hearted lions to breed
experimental ligers and tions as they breed pomatoes and
    totatoes
in botancial gardens.

Eight-foot tigers yawn away their potency. Till yesterday,
   they

burned bright in the forests of the night. It was a way of
living. Now their eyes are embers in the ash. A slight
    movement
of the eyelash flicks the ash.

The other day in Mysore a chimp named Subbu was para-
    lyzed neck
down. He couldn't lift his chipped blue enamel mug to his
    lips
and slurp his tea any more nor pout his lips to puff at his
cigar.

The Society of Animal Lovers babysat for Subbu in shifts till
    in
the small hours of the third morning he bit the sweetest lady
    of
them all in his fury his protectors could not understand.

Lord of lion face, boar snout, and fish eyes, killer of killer
cranes, shepherd of rampant elephants, devour my lambs,
    devour
them whole, save them in the zoo garden ark of your belly.

How It Goes On

MAXINE KUMIN

Today I trade my last unwise
ewe lamb, the one who won't leave home,
for two cords of stove-length oak
and wait on the old enclosed
front porch to make the swap.
November sun revives the thick
trapped buzz of horseflies. The siren
for noon and forest fires blows
a sliding scale. The lamb of woe
looks in at me through glass
on the last day of her life.

Geranium scraps from the window box
trail from her mouth, burdock burrs
are stickered to her fleece like chicken pox,
under her tail stub, permanent smears.

I think of how it goes on,
this dark particular bent of our hungers;
the way a wire eats into a tree
year after year on the pasture's perimeter,
keeping the milk cows penned
until they grow too old to freshen;
of how the last wild horses were scoured
from canyons in Idaho, roped, thrown,
their nostrils twisted shut with wire
to keep them down, the mares aborting,
days later, all of them carted to town.

I think of how it will be
January, nights so cold
the pond cracks like target practice,

daylight glue-colored, sleet falling,
my yellow horse slick with the ball-bearing
sleet, raising up from his dingy browse
out of boredom and habit
to strip bark from the fenced-in trees;
of February, month of the hard palate,
the split wood running out,
worms working in the flour bin.

The lamb, whose time has come, goes off
in the cab of the dump truck, tied to the seat
with baling twine, durable enough
to bear her to the knife and rafter.

O lambs! The whole wolf-world sits down to eat
and cleans its muzzle after.

Horses

MURILO MENDES

Horses gallop over the vast plain.
Going where?
Going to look for the head of the Dauphin that is rolling
      down the stairs.
The spirited horses shake out their long blue manes.
One holds in his teeth the dead white actress he drew from
      the waters,
Others carry the wind's message to vanished explorers,
Others carry wheat to people abandoned by their leaders.
The lean blue horses whinny toward the airplane,
Pound the hard earth with their shining hooves.
They are the last of an old race, man's companion.
He will replace them with mechanical horses
And throw them off into the abyss of history.
The impatient blue horses have closed off the curve of
      the horizon,
Wakening trumpets in the dawn.

translated by W. S. Merwin

Little Elegy with Books and Beasts

(In Memory of Martin Provenson, 1916–1987)

NANCY WILLARD

1

Winters when the gosling froze to its nest
he'd warm it and carry it into the house praising
its finely engraved wings and ridiculous beak,
or sit all night by the roan mare, wrapping
her bruised leg, rinsing the cloths while his wife
read aloud from *Don Quixote*, and darkness hung
on the cold steam of her breath,
or spend five days laying a ladder for the hen
to walk dry-shod into the barn.

Now the black cat broods on the porch.
Now the spotted hound, meeting visitors, greets none.
Nestler, nurse, mender of wounded things
he said he didn't believe in the body.
He lost the gander, elder of all their beasts
(not as wise as the cat but more beloved),
the night of the first frost, the wild geese
calling—last seen waddling south
on the highway, beating his clipped wings.

2

He stepped outside through the usual door
and saw for the last time his bare maples
scrawling their cold script on the low hills
and the sycamore mottled as old stone
and the willows slurred into gold by the spring light,
and he noted the boy clearing the dead brush—

82

old boughs that broke free under the cover of snow—
and he raised his hand, and a door in the air opened,
and what was left of him stumbled and fell
and lay at rest on the earth like a clay lamp
still warm whose flame was not nipped or blown
but lifted out by the one who lit it
and carried alive over the meadow—
that light by which we read, while he was here,
the chapter called Joy in the Book of Creation.

The Sabbath

W. H. AUDEN

Walking on the Seventh Day of Creation,
  They cautiously sniffed the air:
The most fastidious nostril among them admitted
  That fellow was no longer there.

Herbivore, parasite, predator scouted,
  Migrants flew fast and far—
Not a trace of his presence: holes in the earth,
  Beaches covered with tar,

Ruins and metallic rubbish in plenty
  Were all that was left to him
Whose birth on the Sixth had made of that day
  An unnecessary interim.

Well, that fellow had never really smelled
  Like a creature who would survive:
No grace, address of faculty like those
  Born on the first Five.

Back, then, at last on a natural economy,
  Now His Impudence was gone,
Looking exactly like what it was,
  The Seventh Day went on.

Beautiful, happy, perfectly pointless . . .
  A rifle's ringing crack
Split their Arcadia wide open, cut
  Their Sabbath nonsense short.

For whom did they think they had been created?
   That fellow was back,
More bloody-minded than they remembered,
   More god-like than they thought.

Shooting Whales

MARK STRAND

When the shoals of plankton
swarmed into St. Margaret's Bay,
turning the beaches pink,
we saw from our place on the hill
the sperm whales feeding,
fouling the nets
in their play,
and breaching clean
so the humps of their backs
rose over the wide sea meadows.

Day after day
we waited inside
for the rotting plankton to disappear.
The smell stilled even the wind,
and the oxen looked stunned,
pulling hay on the slope
of our hill.
But the plankton kept coming in
and the whales would not go.

That's when the shooting began.
The fishermen got in their boats
and went after the whales,
and my father and uncle
and we children went, too.
The froth of our wake sank fast
in the wind-shaken water.

The whales surfaced close by.
Their foreheads were huge,
the doors of their faces were closed.

Before sounding, they lifted
their flukes into the air
and brought them down hard.
They beat the sea into foam,
and the path that they made
shone after them.

Though I did not see their eyes,
I imagined they were
like the eyes of mourning,
glazed with rheum,
watching us, sweeping along
under the darkening sheets of salt.

When we cut our engine and waited
for the whales to surface again,
the sun was setting,
turning the rock-strewn barrens a gaudy salmon.
A cold wind flailed at our skin.
When finally the sun went down
and it seemed like the whales had gone,
my uncle, no longer afraid,
shot aimlessly into the sky.

Three miles out
in the rolling dark
under the moon's astonished eyes,
our engine would not start
and we headed home in the dinghy.
And my father, hunched over the oars,
brought us in. I watched him,
rapt in his effort, rowing against the tide,

his blond hair glistening with salt.
I saw the slick spillage of moonlight
being blown over his shoulders,
and the sea and spindrift
suddenly silver.

He did not speak the entire way.

At midnight
when I went to bed,
I imagined the whales
moving beneath me,
sliding over the weed-covered hills of the deep;
they knew where I was;
they were luring me
downward and downward
into the murmurous
waters of sleep.

Adam Naming the Creatures

SUZANNE BERGER

My tongue, the new spade to dig through
the acres of namelessness,
Genesis's lush and dreaming mud.
In exhalation, there will be names.
In logos, dominion and order.
Word-skins to call the creatures
in the cacaphony of spinning dark:

You will be *Snail, I am who I carry,*
I am who I shield, with tentacles quivering
in sleep on the Hiddekel's oozing banks.
And you, the sister called *Turtle,*
who wears a leathery sadness,
whose labor rocks out a glisten of eggs,
small moons for these first nights.

And *Fox,* his fur burnished by hot wind,
he lies down, flashing blue-white tendons,
his teeth a snare for the grape and the meat.
He broods over a rookery
of feather-sticks, who are *Birds,*
the grass of prehistory in their claws.

Birds, with wings that flash through the sky,
do you weave air out of yourselves,
or does the air extrude you
to this wildest, speckled firmament?
Free, free, free, you clatter:
Who looks at you shall be moved with flight.

And *Bear,* ursus, the brown-gummed dreamer
eating up his own fat
in the stinking chamber of winter sleep:
he who consumes himself, yet lives,
who wakes up with hunger smeared
on his dripping jaws.

And I, frail bone shaking in this new world,
I live by my syllables and vowels
that, rising, richochet through
the glare of palmettos.
With the fat and protein of these words,
I increase myself, attaching names
like second carapaces, shells and fins.
The cosmos thrums, beating with the noise
of flying and crouching,
their hissing and climbing.

You will be *Bats,* flutter-mice,
with greasy sails on finger bones,
whose upside down sleep
invades our like an incubus,
innocents with defiled and defiling faces.
Fly quietly past *Giraffe*
of the long blue tongue,
past *Walrus,* who walks on her own tusks.

And *Whale,* out there on the seething waters,
with mound shaped like desire,
who bleeds grey to color the ocean,

whose bright saliva is the waves' crest:
contralto, warbler in the longest miles
of opera, muted under fathoms.

And how shall I describe the carrion?
Or the creature of coiled knowledge
that crept into me
on its diamond-studded back?
Through time, I shall bruise its head,
and it shall bruise my heel.

And you I call *Beaver, I am teeth that grow forever,*
who must always gnaw them down —
or mouth-blocked, die in all the streams.
Pity such a killing growth
that would starve by its own vigor.

And poised near the streams are *Deer,*
evanescents, with eyes
the very cups of trembling,
whose tails glow like new clouds,
as they graze on ferns rooting deep
in the shock of this rising sun.

And you, tainted black pig of the world,
understand that we —
the tribe of sky-searching,
upward-walking shafts of flesh —
we will never love you.
You must drag across the world,

this sty of pain,
by your own haunches, your own dumb bulk,
past pitch and tar and slime,
while we lurch above you,
spectators of the animal chaos,
and all that is animal within—
while we watch you rut and bask and lie
in the green carbon forest,
denying that the shine of grime
in your scarred eyes
is the grimy light in ours:
Oh son, misbegotten, oh daughter, ours.

The Leopard-Nurser

JOSEPHINE JACOBSEN

Since children hear what they will hear, I heard
a man had gone to nurse the leopards.
"Women go?"
I asked, and "yes" they said, marveling
in admiration. I envied more than I admired.
Ah! the speechless hurt great leopards
in their woe.

I would go. In a round starry cave
of leaves and moss the green-eyed patients lay;
some worse
than savaged, some bloody, some unmarked:
each beautiful, fluid and fatal
to all save me, their skilled
and speechless nurse.

Though I grew up and went my daylight ways
I never lost that cave. I learned,
at secret length,
that any pain, or any love, reminds me:
a leopard-nurser's is a *métier*
by which a child nurses a dangerous beast
to strength.

FRATERNITY

"Animals Are Only Human"
(a group of mummers).

Pray for the animals, you that pray, you that beg for

mercy, for success and for peace, / the immanent spirit

has also been poured unto them, / they are also souls,

more complete than you, / and clear, brave, beautiful;

and if we begin from the beginning, who knows, / we

shall have to share also these sufferings, / simpler, more

severe, more unlimited than ours.

EEVA-LIISA MANNER

Fraternity is the most complex of the relationships we are looking at, and certainly the most controversial. Are we half-ape, half-angel? The "glory, jest and riddle of the world"? "Half-dust, half-deity"? Where do we fit in the matrix of creation? These questions are not academic, but recur in the literature of each generation—recently, in Desmond Morris's *The Naked Ape,* Michael Fox's *Between Animal and Man,* Lorus and Margery Milne's *The Animal in Man,* Mary Midgley's *Animals and Why They Matter,* and Barry Lopez's *Of Wolves and Men,*[1] to name but a few. Who, in the most literal sense, are our relations, and what are the parameters of our familial attachments? What generates feelings of fraternity among species?

Although Aristotle, the Church Fathers, and many subsequent theologians and philosophers have argued that the animal does not possess a soul and is, therefore, radically different from us, literature as well as life reveals that we *feel* otherwise.

97

The myth of the expulsion of Adam and Eve from the Garden of Eden, in which, legend has it, some animals chose to follow the first parents into exile, is central to Judeo-Christian thinking. In one blow, humankind was alienated not only from God, but from nature itself. Adam and Eve will return to dust, outside Eden, just as miscreants in Greek drama were buried outside the city walls. This forever-exile, this condition of permanent displacement, makes us hungry for fraternity, a need we demonstrate in our use of metaphor to overcome separation and establish connections. When we employ metaphor to describe ourselves in natural images, terms from the nonhuman world, we create unity where division was apparent, reorganizing differences into new likenesses. We say, "It is the east, and Juliet is the sun," or "My love is like a red, red rose," or "A tiger's heart wrapped in a woman's hide," or "Hector is as a lion," or a man is "stubborn as a mule," knitting together a world experienced as fragmentary.

It would be almost impossible to overestimate the influence in literature of the fraternal bond between human and animal. If as citizens of the machine age and consumer societies we enshrine technology and worship manufactured objects, we have by no means abandoned or even transferred our older bonds with animals. We are, despite the incursion of the machine into all spheres of our lives, unable to view it as kindred. It remains matter, whereas we are matter and something more. The machine may serve us, but it cannot love us. By contrast, we do have a powerful inherited notion which nourishes us: we belong to and are part of the animal world.

Fraternal feelings between kind and kind are present from the beginning of history; in *The Gilgamesh Epic,* written before the Bible, we find the passage:

> Gilgamesh was called a god and man.
> Enkidu was called animal and man.
> It is the story
> of their being human together.

We know, too, that in the poems of Eskimos, Native Americans, Africans, and other peoples whose oral and early written literature has not been destroyed, there is an assertion of a common ancestry for man and animal. Such a belief lies behind the prayer of the Kiva Indians, who before a deer hunt plead for forgiveness: "For we are all bound together, and our touch upon one travels through all to return to us again. Let us not forget the deer." Such a view suggests a tie even closer than that which resulted in the "gifting" of dominion or the animal worship of reverence; it is a sense of fellow-feeling.

Similarly, African legend has it that the early hunters after killing their prey made a practice of turning their bows around to change the stringing tension in them, then used them as musical instruments. The music played was intended as an act of atonement, to bring peace to the spirit of the animals who had nourished these human beings with their flesh. Thousands of miles away in Japan, in a very early poem, "Sorrows for the Deer," we find a stag exacting tribute from his hunter: "Then praise, praise me to the skies!" This animistic view of the world (that both creatures and objects of nature are inhabited by spirits and that the *spirit,* not the body, is the true being), is pervasive in archaic societies. Such a view created a feeling of coherence; archaic people and their environment were one. In this, they were more fortunate than we.

Mircea Eliade, a renowned historian of religion, reminds us that in such societies a person knows that he or she can die and come back to life, that sacred sexual acts and other rituals can influence crops, that ancestors were animals.

The Native American poet Helen Knopf, in "Memories" (1977), writes about certain routes and watering places of the Indians, "even when we was all animals / we stopped there."

Fraternal feelings between human and animal, however, are not peculiar to certain societies nor exclusive to the past. This theme endures through the centuries, going through cultural permutations but never vanishing. Poets like Crabbe, Cowley, and Clare in the English pastoral tradition wrote visually descriptive poetry about animals which resembles the contemporary poetry of Ted Hughes *(Season Songs)* and Maxine Kumin. In such work, both past and present, human life participates in a celebration of the seasons of nature, brought near to us by observing the cyclical roles of other creatures. "Summer is y-comen in, / Loude, sing cuckoo!" exclaims the lyric, intertwining season and birdsong. We still mark the arrival and departure of birds and animals, change in coloration and growth of trees, even though today most of us do not labor according to nature's time, the time of cycles and seasons, of organic growth, as when Hesiod wrote *Works and Days* and Spenser *The Shepheardes Calendar.*

Even in the eighteenth century, the Age of Reason, which interpreted the world as a Great Chain of Being where everything connected vertically and fixedly with man at the pinnacle, Alexander Pope cautioned: "And just as short of reason he must fall / Who thinks all [creatures] made for one [man] not one for all." However, in general, the eighteenth century before the pre-Romantics was a period of schism and of separation of humans from nature, resulting in poetic artificialities such as the personification of, and direct address to, natural forces — Wind, Air, Rain, and so on — substituting for particularized, observed description. Such poetic connection with nature seems to the contemporary reader as impersonal, distant, and as overly contrived as many eighteenth-century formal gardens.

However, with the rise of the Romantic poets of the late eighteenth and the nineteenth centuries, there came a strong reemphasis on fraternal bonding between people and animals. Poets like Blake, Wordsworth, Shelley, Cowper, and Burns come immediately to mind. And when William Blake begins his poem "The Fly" with the question "Am I not a fly like you?" he anticipates by more than a hundred years "Gnat-Psalm" by his fellow Englishman Ted Hughes. In Hughes's poem, the insects are described not only as capable of reaching human heights, but also heights few humans do achieve, "singing and dancing in a religious ecstasy." Both Blake and Hughes, by comparing themselves to insignificant and diminutive insects, emphasize in startling fashion the oneness of creation.

This unitary view receives scientific validation; for example, a Harvard entomologist, V. B. Wigglesworth, in his *Life of Insects,* declares, "Insects are not curiosities; they are creatures in common with ourselves, bound by the law's decree that everything alive must live by observing the same elemental principles that make life."[2] And Darwin's own image for evolution was a branching bush, a horizontal growth, not the vertical Chain of Being. This nonhierarchical image is a crucial one for fraternity.

Furthermore, poets reflect that animals don't suffer from some of our congenital human flaws; they do have abilities we can't emulate. So Whitman muses, "I could turn and live with the animals," finding them refreshingly free from human discontent, pomposity, and whining. Hughes's "Gnat-Psalm" carries on this interesting perspective: the gnats are praised for what they *don't* do that we *do* do, "writing and fighting," as well as for doing what we *can't* do: they can "hear the wind suffering," "the towns saddening," "the wind bowing," just as the Portuguese poet Carlos Drummond de Andrade sees the elephant able to "walk the battlefield without crushing plants." Marianne Moore, who has written many of the finest animal poems of this century, salutes the animals for "minding their own business," and because they "do not make us self-conscious." Unlike some people, they do not have "the passion for setting people right."

So the animals are worthy, even exemplary brothers. "Go to the ant . . . consider her ways and be wise," says Proverbs.

Nineteenth-century Darwinian biology provided a scientific basis for breaking down species barriers, twentieth-century Freudianism added its own confirming theories about human nature and its animal affinities. Psychoanalyst Carl Gustav Jung delved deeply into the animal archetypes of human dreams; his followers are still pursuing this line of inquiry. Boundaries between species are now generally conceded to be fluid; beasts are not strange, but kin. Konrad Lorenz argued in his study *On Aggression*[3] that human aggression is an instinct, not a learned reaction; moreover, he claimed that animals are less likely than human beings to fight to the death. As a consequence of new scientific and ethnological studies of behavior, we do seem today to be forging horizontal, rather than vertical, connections to other creatures. Contemporary consciousness is more averse to imposing an anthropomorphic and anthropocentric vision upon the world. "As post-Darwinians it [is] up to us to anthropomorphize the world less, and animalize, vegetablize, and mineralize ourselves more," advises contemporary poet Galway Kinnell.

Such empathic extensions of ourselves as Kinnell calls for would reintroduce possibilities of transformation, metamorphosis, between kind and kind such as Homer, Virgil, Ovid, and Plato familiarly drew upon. Transformational notions continue to permeate some cultures, such as that of the American Plains Indians ("Materialized into an Owl" is the title of a poem by the Native American Louis Little Coon Oliver). Poems written today by the Inuit include many such persona poems of animals and birds, because their culture accepts a metamorphic tradition, freeing the poet to speak in the voice of another creature. Scientific understanding, however, has largely rendered this tradition suspect, except to the artistic imagination.[4] Transformational possibility is recaptured in W. B. Yeats's "The Song of Wandering Aengus":

> I dropped the berry in a stream
> And caught a little silver trout.

> When I had laid it on the floor
> I went to blow the fire aflame,
> But something rustled on the floor,
> And some one called me by my name:
> It had become a glimmering girl
> With apple blossom in her hair
> Who called me by my name and ran.

or Derek Walcott's lines concluding "Midsummer XXXIX":

> that my bastard ancestor swayed
> transfixed by the trembling, trembling thing that stood
> its ground, ears pronged, nibbling him into a hare.

We accept transformations of physical being as signs of developmental process—we age, stoop, our hair turns gray, and so on. But we have lost belief in those possibilities of transformation that the masks, cloaks, hair adornments, and makeup of Indian and African ritual dancing bespeak. People in these cultures retain a direct relation to transformation; they can become "other" because they are not limited to seeing "other" only as metaphor for oneself.

Most obviously, what we *share* with animals in the fraternal relation is the condition of mortality; for this reason, Robert Frost can appropriate an oven*bird* to pose the problem of *human* aging: "what to make of a diminished thing." Although we have prior knowledge of our end and animals don't, *we* see it as the common fate. The Bible instructs us in this commonality: "For the fate of man is as that of the beasts—and as a beast he draws breath, and as a beast dies so does he." The travel writer Jan Morris, in her book on Spain, informs us that the matador, "with a graceful and brotherly hand," strokes his dying adversary between the horns where the blade is lodged. As the twentieth-century philosopher Alfred North Whitehead summarizes, the inescapable condition of being is "the witness of the body." The body is our mortal part, and it is nowhere if not with us; without it, we cannot be.

Delmore Schwartz's "The Heavy Bear" reveals in its first line, "The heavy bear who goes with me," the burdensome notion of the animal/body, and John Logan also focuses on this particular bond of the frail flesh. Logan explicitly states in his poem "The Zoo": "How much my life is a human life, / my death an animal death." And Borges addresses "The White Deer" of his dream, "I too am dream, lasting a few days longer." Such recognition of cosubstantiality is exactly why the practice of animal sacrifice, going back at least as far in recorded history as Roman state religion, could work as an imaginative substitution. The animal scapegoat depends upon the animal being perceived as a close enough approximation of the human to function as an imaginative substitution.

Obviously Darwin's work on evolution not only substantiated feelings of relationship among creatures, it also raised questions that still deeply trouble traditional concepts of human superiority. The famous "monkey trial" of 1925 centered on whether a teacher in the Tennessee public school system should be allowed to teach evolution; Scopes, the defendant, lost the case, and that decision was not rescinded until 1967! Later the Louisiana legislature passed a bill requiring that creationism be taught along with evolution, a decision that was finally reversed by a U.S. appellate court in June 1987. Though the creationists represent an extreme of religious opinion, philosophical problems connected to evolutionary theory may arise for all of us. How do we balance the scientific explanation of "fitness" as the criterion for survival and evolution against religious ideas that set moral goals uppermost? And what happens to our visual iconography of an anthropomorphic supreme deity?

In fact, Darwin, in *The Expression of Emotion in Man and Animals*,[5] went even further, proposing that an instructive analysis and comparison could take place between human and animal emotions as manifest in their countenances. His contention was that human facial expressions are the visible remains of what were once necessary, purposive facial changes for the animal, for example, the symbolic freezing, grimacing, lip-curling response to physical threat. There is, of course, marked revulsion on the part of some to the idea of such close connectedness. Animals may trigger images of bestiality, particularly grossness, greed, cruelty. In such responses, a binary opposition is established in the mind of the respondent between the category "human," which connotes "humane," and animal, which connotes "bestial," though, in fact, the *Oxford English Dictionary* supplies no such distinction, defining "bestial" merely as "a living being including mammals, birds, fishes, insects and reptiles."

Identification with animal being need not signify loss of control, irrationality, or self-loathing, as it seems to in Schwartz's "The Heavy Bear" or Philip Levine's "Animals Are Passing from Our Lives." The recognition of an animal self does not have to be degrading, though that interpretation received strong support from Puritanism in America and Calvinism in Europe. The attributes on which we base our identification reflect our own choices. We can invest fraternity with the reassurance of fellowship such as we find, for example, in Jacopo Bassano's painting *The Flood,* where human and animal destiny join together to enter the Ark.

A Robert Lowell sonnet for his daughter, "Harriet," moves easily between "them" and "us," building upon the observation that the young of any species share the qualities of youth—a playfulness and energy that transcend species distinctions. Here is an excerpt from the fourth sonnet of the sequence:

> To summer on skidding summer, the rude spring rain
> hurries the ambitious, flowers and youth;
> the crackling flash-tone's held an hour, then we
> too follow nature, imperceptibly
> change from mouse-brown to white lion's mane,
> to thin white, to the freckled, knuckled skull,
> bronzed by decay, by many, many suns . . .
> The child of ten, three quarters animal,
> three years from Juliet, half Juliet,
> already ripens for the night on stage—

We share not only mortality with animals, but developmental stages, social organization, and even traits of temperament. For instance, in Eugenio Montale's book of poems *Flashes and Dedications,* the volume's heroine, Clizia, Beatrice to his Dante, represents a carnality which Montale views as quite compatible with the radiance of transcendence. And this female figure is represented, at various points in the poem, as a personal totemic animal of her lover's, a vixen, trout, dove, zebu, okapi. And Marina Tsvetayeva compares her lover's rejection to the wounding of a beast in "Poem of the End" (9):

> here is the sacred and sublingual
> secret wives keep from their husbands and

widows from friends, here is the full
story Eve took from the tree:
I am no more than an animal that
someone has stabbed in the stomach.
translated by Elaine Feinstein

Without a fundamental assumption of likeness, there could be
no transference, no lessons in animal stories and fables, because,
of course, while they are about animals they are *for* us. Books
such as Chaucer's *Parliament of Fowles,* Canto I of Dante's *In-
ferno,* Jonson's drama *Volpone,* Mandeville's *Fable of the Bees,*
Gray's poem "Ode on the Death of a Favorite Cat," Swift's
Gulliver's Travels, and Günter Grass's *The Flounder* and *The
Rat* all depend upon this similitude, describing us as animals both
in our individual and social relations, because through animal
fables we can plumb our own natures. X. J. Kennedy's humorous
poems about animals, like Leigh Hunt's and T. S. Eliot's, even
help accommodate us to our physical oddities; the wart on the
hog is easier to accept than the wart on our own noses; the
dachshund's stubby legs, the waddling goose enable us to view
as comedic our own shortcomings. "Bedraggled Ostrich," pathetic
foolish bird in a zoo, gradually impresses itself upon the contemporary Japanese poet Takamura Kotaro as more and more
human until the poem's climax, "Isn't it no longer an ostrich /
More a man?" Fraternity teaches us that animals are a double
metaphor for humankind; the best and worst in us find correspondence. The clearest glimpse we have of ourselves is another's
face in the mirror.

Just as in the past, in our own time this resemblance serves
satiric, political ends. Disguised by the adoption of animal characters, a message of danger can be disseminated, the mighty
mocked. For example, Orwell's classic *Animal Farm,* the Russian comic strip *Krokodil,* and the poem "The Monkeys at Hardwar" expose systems of colonialism and dictatorship by employing
animal actors who personify political oppressors. In T. S. Eliot's
parodic poem "The Hippopotamus," that mucky animal is washed

clean by angels and ascends to heaven, while the Church remains below "wrapt in its miasmal mist."

The fact that animals can serve a didactic end underlines the degree to which we are able to see their world as ours. Perhaps the most striking contemporary example of this is Art Spiegelman's *Maus: A Survivor's Tale* (1986),[6] the story of Holocaust victims in Poland in which Jews are depicted as mice, Nazis as cats, and Poles as pigs. All the great animal fables, such as those of La Fontaine or Aesop, contain lessons for life, and are certainly not limited to juvenile audiences.

Still, we do first come to animals in early childhood: *Mother Goose* and *The Oxford Book of Nursery Rhymes,* Perrault and *Peter and the Wolf.* Through stories and verses with animal protagonists, children catch glimpses of a practical world in which grownups go "to market, to market, to buy a fat pig." They learn of a moral world in which "Pussy won't hurt me if I do her no harm." They feel the exigencies of a natural world in which winter threatens "poor Robin." Within the classification "Books for Juveniles," no other single source provides so many characters as the animal world. These animal characters are based upon an implicit recognition of fraternity so powerful in children that they even accept the convention of talking animals, as in such perennial favorites as *Winnie-the-Pooh* and *The Wind in the Willows.* Some books establish the fraternal connection firmly in the title: *Brer* (Brother) Fox and *Uncle* Wiggly. Others relate tales of extraordinary fidelity of dog to child. This phenomenon of the special relationship between children and animals reveals a great fund of empathy which we carry with us into adulthood.[7]

Children learn from animals their first lesson in the idea of love, a crucial model for future development. Indeed, bonding with animals is seen almost as a stage in the evolution of the affections:

> Why did the lamb love Mary so?
> The eager children cry.
> Why, Mary loves the lamb, you know,
> The teacher did reply.

That love will, in the course of time, be transferred to human beings. As Jon Silkin writes today in "Caring for Animals":

Attend to the unnecessary beasts.

From growing mercy and a moderate love
Great love for the human animal occurs.

And your love grows. Your great love grow and grows.

Acknowledgment of the fraternal bond among creatures and of a mutuality of responsibility makes possible the positive power of love's intercession and the alleviation of suffering. As children we read how heroes and heroines are advanced in their perilous quests by animal helpers, a well-defined motif in folk and fairy tales.[8] We seek the same succor as adults. Eskimo carvings from the Dorset culture depict polar bears aiding shamans to escape their bodies and enter the spirit world, even accompanying them to the spirit world. Similarly, the sculptures of the Huichol Indians of Mexico's west coast represent dogs and parrots guiding humans to the nether world. Conversely, humans are efficacious helpers when they act through love; when Beauty kisses the frog, he is transformed into a Prince. This story, in fact, belongs to a whole subcategory of fairy tales employing the animal-bride-groom plot, and in each case the lesson purveyed is the magical potency of love to effect change. This is the tradition from which Galway Kinnell's poem "Kissing the Toad" derives; the toad "watches the girl who might kiss it, / pisses, quakes, tries / to make its smile wider: / *to love on, oh yes, to love on.*"

The flow of compassion among creatures, even more strongly rooted in Eastern than in Western cultures, is emblematized in the Jataka tales of Buddha's former animal and human lives in which animals sacrifice themselves for people, and people for animals. As readers, the comfort and consolation we derived in childhood from fairy-tale helpers we find anew in poetry about the fraternal bond. For example, Derek Walcott's poem "The Season of Phantasmal Peace" imagines that birds, pitying "the wingless ones" . . . lift the net of the world until "there was no longer dusk, or season, decline or weather," while William Stafford in "The Animal that Drank Up Sound" ascribes the rebirth of sound in a world gone mute to crickets rubbing their legs together for all our sakes.

The mutuality of the fraternal bond is displayed nowhere more prominently than in the practice of keeping pets. Although at first glance the keeping of domestic animals might seem to belong more to the caretaking relation of dominion than to fraternity, the intensity of the human/animal bonding that can occur belies that interpretation. Does it strike us as peculiar to have bequests left in wills to animal beneficiaries? This is only the furthest extension of the common practice of regarding domestic animals, as many pet-lovers do, as "one of the family." When one comes to think of it, is it not an oddity to have an animal cemetery in Paris? Especially since, unlike the early Egyptians who built a cat cemetery in the ancient town of Beni Hasan, in France animals are not held to be agents of supernatural power. This latter-day Parisian cemetery does not monumentalize reverence, but affection. Perhaps this is not so strange when one thinks of other ways in which such affectionate ties have been extravagantly displayed: *Flush,* Elizabeth Barrett Browning's dog memorialized in prose by Virginia Woolf; Carpaccio's famous painting of courtesans in Venice fondling their dogs as they idle their time between customers. And what of the lapdogs left free to run upon the dining table in the *Très Riches Heures?* If Chinese court ladies carried pet Pekingese in the wide sleeves of their robes, sailors commonly perched parrots on their shoulders. Marmosets and capuchin monkeys turn up in art as domestic pets. Hogarth with his pet bull terrier is captured for history by the painter himself. These visual and literary portraits appeal directly to our emotions; we understand instinctively the fraternal bond that is portrayed. Indeed, in our own time, psychologists and anthropologists have focused attention on the human/pet relationship and its significance, finding surprising correlations between health, both mental and physical, and human interaction with pets.[9]

Through the relation of fraternity, allegories and fables teach us about ourselves and at the same time bestow the gift of connectedness to other creatures, extending kinship and affection which mitigate our human loneliness. Fraternity liberates a human imagination fettered by political frontiers, egocentricism, and the prevailing analytical habit of polarization, all of which ignore the fact that nature itself is indivisible, interdependent, and interactive. The fraternal attitude, sharpened and intensified today, has roots in "praise poems" such as Christopher Smart's "Jubilate Agno" and "Of Jeoffrey, My Cat"—poems of reunion with nature and with other creatures. The spirit of fraternity, in the fullness of its meaning, is captured in a classic rejoinder by Thoreau: asked why, if he wanted to study birds, he didn't shoot one, but was content with birdwatching, he quipped, "Do you think I would shoot you if I wanted to study you?"

The Chance to
Love Everything

MARY OLIVER

All summer I made friends
with the creatures nearby—
they flowed through the fields
and under the tent walls,
or padded through the door,
grinning through their many teeth,
looking for seeds,
suet, sugar; muttering and humming,
opening the breadbox, happiest when
there was milk and music. But once
in the night I heard a sound
outside the door, the canvas
bulged slightly—something
was pressing inward at eye level.
I watched, trembling, sure I had heard
the click of claws, the smack of lips
outside my gauzy house—
I imagined the red eyes,
the broad tongue, the enormous lap.
Would it be friendly too?
Fear defeated me. And yet,
not in faith and not in madness
but with the courage I thought
my dream deserved,
I stepped outside. It was gone.
Then I whirled at the sound of some
shambling tonnage.
Did I see a black haunch slipping
back through the trees? Did I see
the moonlight shining on it?

Did I actually reach out my arms
toward it, toward paradise falling, like
the fading of the dearest, wildest hope—
the dark heart of the story that is all
the reason for its telling?

Sonnet of Intimacy

VINÍCIUS DE MORAES

Farm afternoons, there's too much blue air.
I go out sometimes, follow the pasture track,
Chewing a blade of sticky grass, chest bare,
In threadbare pajamas of three summers back,

To the little rivulets in the river-bed
For a drink of water, cold and musical,
And if I spot in the brush a glow of red,
A raspberry, spit its blood at the corral.

The smell of cow manure is delicious.
The cattle look at me unenviously
And when there comes a sudden stream and hiss

Accompanied by a look not unmalicious,
All of us, animals, unemotionally
Partake together of a pleasant piss.

translated by Elizabeth Bishop

Caring for Animals

JON SILKIN

I ask sometimes why these small animals
With bitter eyes, why we should care for them.

I question the sky, the serene blue water,
But it cannot say. It gives no answer.

And no answer releases in my head
A procession of grey shades patched and whimpering.

Dogs with clipped ears, wheezing cart horses
A fly without shadow and without thought.

Is it with these menaces to our vision
With this procession led by a man carrying wood

We must be concerned? The holy land, the rearing
Green island should be kindlier than this.

Yet the animals, our ghosts, need tending to.
Take in the whipped cat and the blinded owl;

Take up the man-trapped squirrel upon your shoulder.
Attend to the unnecessary beasts.

From growing mercy and a moderate love
Great love for the human animal occurs.

And your love grows. Your great love grows and
grows.

The Bat

THEODORE ROETHKE

By day the bat is cousin to the mouse.
He likes the attic of an aging house.

His fingers make a hat about his head.
His pulse beat is so slow we think him dead.

He loops in crazy figures half the night
Among the trees that face the corner light.

But when he brushes up against a screen,
We are afraid of what our eyes have seen:

For something is amiss or out of place
When mice with wings can wear a human face.

In Monument Valley

JAMES MERRILL

One spring twilight, during a lull in the war,
At Shroup's farm south of Troy, I last rode horseback.
Stillnesses were swarming inward from the evening star
Or outward from the bouyant sorrel mare

Who moved as if not displeased with the weight upon her.
Meadows received us, heady with unseen lilac.
Brief polyphonic lives abounded everywhere.
With one accord we circled the small lake.

Yet here I sit among the crazy shapes things take.
Wasp-waisted to a fault by long abrasion,
The "Three Sisters" howl. "Hell's Gate" yawns wide.
I'm eating something in the cool Hertz car

When the shadow falls. There has come to my door
As to death's this creature stunted, cinder-eyed,
Tottering still half in trust, half in fear of man—
Dear god, a horse. I offer my apple-core

But she is past hunger, she lets it roll in the sand,
And I, I raise the window and drive on.
About the ancient bond between her kind and mine
Little more to speak of can be done.

Animals

ROBINSON JEFFERS

At dawn a knot of sea-lions lies off the shore
In the slow swell between the rock and cliff,
Sharp flippers lifted, or great-eyed heads, as they roll in the sea,
Bigger than draft-horses, and barking like dogs,
Their all-night song. It makes me wonder a little
That life near kin to human, intelligent, hot-blooded,
   idle and singing, can float with ease
In the ice-cold midwinter water. Then yellow dawn
Colors the south, I think about the rapid and furious lives
   in the sun:
They have little to do with ours; they have nothing to do with
   oxygen and salted water; they would look monstrous

If we could see them: the beautiful passionate bodies of living
Flame, beastlike flapping and screaming,
Tortured with burning lust and acute awareness, that ride the
   storm-tides
Of the great fire-globe. They are animals, as we are. There are
   many other chemistries of animal life
Besides the slow oxidation of carbohydrates and amino acids.

The Lion in Love

MARIANNE MOORE

Mademoiselle—goddess instead—
In whom the Graces find a school
Although you are more beautiful,
Even if with averted head,
Might you not be entertained
By a tale that is unadorned—
Hearing with no more than a quiver
Of a lion whom Love knew how to conquer.
Love is a curious mastery,
In name alone a felicity.
Better know of than know the thing.
If too personal and thus trespassing,
I'm saying what may seem to you an offense,
A fable could not offend your ear.
This one, assured of your lenience,
Attests its devotion embodied here,
And kneels in sworn obedience.

Before their speech was obstructed,
Lions or such as were attracted
To young girls, sought an alliance.
Why not? since as paragons of puissance,
They were at that time knightly fellows
Of mettle and intelligence
Adorned by manes like haloes.

The point of the preamble follows.
A lion—one in a multitude—
Met in a meadow as he fared,
A shepherdess for whom he cared.
He sought to win her if he could,
Though the father would have preferred

A less ferocious son-in-law.
To consent undoubtedly was hard;
Fear meant that the alternate was barred.
Moreover, refuse and he foresaw
That some fine day the two might explain
Clandestine marriage as the chain
That fettered the lass, bewitched beyond cure,
By fashions conducive to hauteur,
And a fancy that shaggy shoulder fur
Made her willful lower handsomer.
The father with despair choked down,
Said though at heart constrained to frown,
"The child is a dainty one; better wait;
You might let your claw points scratch her
When your heavy forepaws touch her.
You could if not too importunate,
Have your claws clipped. And there in front,
See that your teeth are filed blunt,
Because a kiss might be enjoyed
By you the more, I should think,
If my daughter were not forced to shrink
Because improvidently annoyed."
The enthralled animal mellowed,
His mind's eye having been shuttered.
Without teeth or claws it followed
That the fortress was shattered.
Dogs were loosed; defenses were gone:
The consequence was slight resistance.

Love, ah Love, when your slipknot's drawn,
We can but say, "Farewell, good sense."

Gnat-Psalm

TED HUGHES

The Gnat is of more ancient lineage than man.
— Proverb

When the gnats dance at evening
Scribbling on the air, sparring sparely,
Scrambling their crazy lexicon,
Shuffling their dumb Cabala,
Under leaf shadow

Leaves only leaves
Between them and the broad thrusts of the sun
Leaves muffling the dusty stabs of the late sun
From their frail eyes and crepuscular temperaments

Dancing
Dancing
Writing on the air, rubbing out everything they
     write
Jerking their letters into knots, into tangles
Everybody everybody else's yoyo

Immense magnets fighting around a centre

Not writing and not fighting but singing
That the cycles of this Universe are not matter
That they are not afraid of the sun
That the one sun is too near
It blasts their song, which is of all the suns
That they are their own sun
Their own brimming over
At large in the nothing

Their wings blurring the blaze
Singing
Singing

That they are the nails
In the dancing hands and feet of the gnat-god
That they hear the wind suffering
Through the grass
And the evening hill suffering
And the towns, camped by their graveyards,
Saddening into an utter darkness

The wind bowing with long cat-gut cries
And highways and airways
Dancing in the wind
The wind's dance, the death-dance,
Plunging into marshes and undergrowth
And cities like cowdroppings huddling to dust

But not the gnats, their agility
Has outleaped that threshold
And hangs them a little above the claws of the
    grass
Dancing
Dancing
In the glove shadows of the sycamore

A dance never to be altered
A dance giving their bodies to be burned

And their mummy faces will never be used

Their little bearded faces
Weaving and bobbing on the nothing
Shaken in the air, shaken, shaken
And their feet dangling like the feet of victims

O little Hasids
Ridden to death by your own bodies
Riding your bodies to death
You are the angels of the only heaven!

And God is an Almighty Gnat!
You are the greatest of all the galaxies!
My hands fly in the air, they are follies
My tongue hangs up in the leaves
My thoughts have crept into crannies

Your dancing

Your dancing

Rolls my staring skull slowly away into outer
    space.

The Bull Returns

YEHUDA AMICHAI

The bull returns after his day of work in the ring
after a cup of coffee with his opponents,
having left them with his address and
the exact location of the red scarf.
The sword remains in his stiff-necked neck.
And when he's usually at home. Now
he sits on his bed, with his heavy
Jewish eyes. He knows
that the sword too is hurt when it pierces flesh.
In his next incarnation he'll be a sword: the hurt will
    remain.
("The door is open. If not, the key is under the mat.")
He knows about the mercy of twilight and about the final
mercy. In the Bible, he's listed with the clean
    animals.
He's very kosher: chews his cud,
and even his heart is divided and cloven like a hoof.
From his chest, hairs burst forth
dry and gray, as though from a split mattress.

The Spider

CÉSAR VALLEJO

It is a huge spider, which can no longer move;
a spider which is colorless, whose body,
a head and an abdomen, is bleeding.

Today I watched it with great care. With what
tremendous energy
to every side
it was stretching out its many feet.
And I have been thinking of its invisible eyes,
and death-bringing pilots of the spider.

It is a spider which was shivering, fixed
on the sharp ridge of a stone;
the abdomen on one side,
and on the other, the head.

With so many feet the poor thing, and still it cannot
solve it! And seeing it
confused in such great danger,
what a great pain that traveler has given me today!

It is a huge spider, whose abdomen
prevents him from following his head.
And I have been thinking of his eyes
and of his many, many feet . . .
And what a strange pain that traveler has given me!

translated by Robert Bly

124

The Heavy Bear

DELMORE SCHWARTZ

The heavy bear who goes with me,
A manifold honey to smear his face,
Clumsy and lumbering here and there,
The central ton of every place,
The hungry beating brutish one
In love with candy, anger, and sleep,
Crazy factotum, dishevelling all,
Climbs the building, kicks the football,
Boxes his brother in the hate-ridden city.

Breathing at my side, that heavy animal,
That heavy bear who sleeps with me,
Howls in his sleep for a world of sugar,
A sweetness intimate as the water's clasp,
Howls in his sleep because the tight-rope
Trembles and shows the darkness beneath.
—The strutting show-off is terrified,
Dressed in his dress-suit, bulging his pants,
Trembles to think that his quivering meat
Must finally wince to nothing at all.

That inescapable animal walks with me,
Has followed me since the black womb held,
Moves where I move, distorting my gesture,
A caricature, a swollen shadow,
A stupid clown of the spirit's motive,
Perplexes and affronts with his own darkness,
The secret life of belly and bone,
Opaque, too near, my private, yet unknown,
Stretches to embrace the very dear
With whom I would walk without him near,
Touches her grossly, although a word

125

Would bare my heart and make me clear,
Stumbles, flounders, and strives to be fed
Dragging me with him in his mouthing care,
Amid the hundred million of his kind,
The scrimmage of appetite everywhere.

An Ox Looks at Man

CARLOS DRUMMOND DE ANDRADE

They are more delicate even than shrubs and they run and
run from one side to the other, always forgetting
something. Surely they lack I don't know what basic
ingredient, though they present themselves as noble or
serious, at times. Oh, terribly serious, even tragic.
Poor things, one would say that they hear neither the
song of air nor the secrets of hay; likewise they seem
not to see what is visible and common to each of us, in
space. And they are sad, and in the wake of sadness
they come to cruelty. All their expression lives in
their eyes—and loses itself to a simple lowering of
lids, to a shadow. And since there is little of the
mountain about them—nothing in the hair or in the
terribly fragile limbs but coldness and secrecy—it is
impossible for them to settle themselves into forms that
are calm, lasting, and necessary. They have, perhaps, a
kind of melancholy grace (one minute) and with this they
allow themselves to forget the problems and translucent
inner emptiness that make them so poor and so lacking
when it comes to uttering silly and painful sounds:
desire, love, jealousy (what do we know?)—sounds that
scatter and fall in the field like troubled stones and
burn the herbs and the water, and after this it is hard
to keep chewing away at our truth.

translated by Mark Strand

Two Horses Playing in the Orchard

JAMES WRIGHT

Too soon, too soon, a man will come
To lock the gate, and drive them home.
Then, neighing softly through the night,
The mare will nurse her shoulder bite.
Now, lightly fair, through lock and mane
She gazes over the dusk again,
And sees her darkening stallion leap
In grass for apples, half asleep.

Lightly, lightly, on slender knees
He turns, lost in a dream of trees.
Apples are slow to find this day,
Someone has stolen the best away.
Still, some remain before the snow,
A few, trembling on boughs so low
A horse can reach them, small and sweet:
And some are tumbling to her feet.

Too soon, a man will scatter them,
Although I do not know his name,
His age, or how he came to own
A horse, an apple tree, a stone.
I let those horses in to steal
On principle, because I feel
Like half a horse myself, although
Too soon, too soon, already. Now.

Monkeys at Hardwar

TAUFIQ RAFAT

One remembers the monkeys at Hardwar,
in the good old days when Bharat was India,
who snatched food from the hands of the unwary.
Being sacred, they plundered with impunity.
We were children then, on our way to Lahore
for the winter break. When we passed Hardwar
we anticipated the monkeys, who perched
in rows on the train-roof awaiting their chance.
We could not see them, but knew they were there
from experience, more sudden and dangerous
than those who chattered on the crowded platform.
There were temples too. Since then, in my mind,
monkeys and temples have been synonymous.

    The only monkeys one sees now
    are in the zoo, or at the end of a chain,
    but they are a poor lot compared
    to those bold, religious monkeys.

One also remembers, with a twinge of regret,
lone Englishmen in first-class carriages,
remote and god-like, and firmly entrenched
behind three month old newspapers from Home.
They kept their teeth clenched on cold pipes
as they carried the Empire to ungodly districts.
Even in the hottest weather their glass-windows
were shut; they took no notice of the monkeys.
Whenever we wanted to appear superior
we imitated their Ur-doo, and secretly lusted
for the memsahibs who came to kiss them goodbye.

They were clean solid fellows in sola hats
who knew how to keep us out of their hair.

The only sahibs one sees now
are the back-slapping oil executives,
or the sleazy christs from Europe
who infest our zebra-crossings.

Animals Are Passing from Our Lives

PHILIP LEVINE

It's wonderful how I jog
on four honed-down ivory toes
my massive buttocks slipping
like oiled parts with each light step.

I'm to market. I can smell
the sour, grooved block, I can smell
the blade that opens the hole
and the pudgy white fingers

that shake out the intestines
like a hankie. In my dreams
the snouts drool on the marble,
suffering children, suffering flies,

suffering the consumers
who won't meet their steady eyes
for fear they could see. The boy
who drives me along believes

that any moment I'll fall
on my side and drum my toes
like a typewriter or squeal
and shit like a new housewife

discovering television,
or that I'll turn like a beast
cleverly to hook his teeth
with my teeth. No. Not this pig.

The Season of Phantasmal Peace

DEREK WALCOTT

Then all the nations of birds lifted together
the huge net of the shadows of this earth
in multitudinous dialects, twittering tongues,
stitching and crossing it. They lifted up
the shadows of the long pines down trackless slopes,
the shadows of glass-faced towers down evening streets,
the shadow of a frail plant on a city sill—
the net rising soundless as night, the birds' cries soundless,
    until
there was no longer dusk, or season, decline or weather,
only this passage of phantasmal light
that not the narrowest shadow dared to sever.

And men could not see, looking up, what the wild geese
    drew,
what the ospreys trailed behind them in silvery ropes
that flashed in the icy sunlight; they could not hear
battalions of starlings waging peaceful cries,
bearing the net higher, covering this world
like the vines of an orchard, or a mother drawing
the trembling gauze over the trembling eyes
of a child fluttering to sleep;
                it was the light
that you will see at evening on the side of a hill
in yellow October, and no one hearing knew
what change had brought into the raven's cawing,
the killdeer's screech, the ember-circling chough,
such an immense, soundless and high concern
for the fields and cities where the birds belong,

except it was their seasonal passing, Love,
made seasonless, or, from the high privilege of their birth,
something brighter than pity for the wingless ones
below them who shared dark holes in windows and in
    houses,
and higher they lifted the net with soundless voices
above all change, betrayals of falling suns,
and this season lasted one moment, like the pause
between dusk and darkness, between fury and peace,
but for such as our earth is now, it lasted long.

COMMUNION

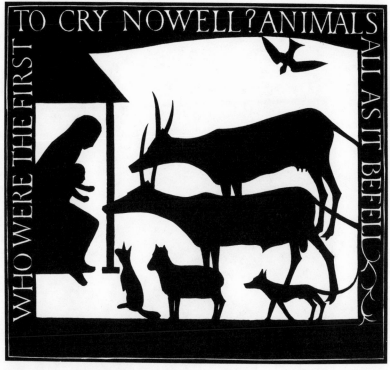

"Who Were The First To Cry Nowell?"
woodcut by Eric Gill.

For I am merely
Quite an ordinary hunter,
Who never inherited song
From the twittering birds of the sky.

"THE SONG OF THE TROUT-FISHER"

IKINILIK

Is there a statement perfect in its
speech?

A. R. AMMONS

Poems move between boundaries, shift and progress into new definitions as strong works of art are bound to do. Therefore, although the poems illustrating the theme of communion might have been equally appropriate in another category of relation, they are grouped together here to focus attention on the fascinating question: What discourse is possible within the sphere of human/animal relations? Then, further, does this relation of communion change what we feel about our human identification with "the word"? We have seen that humankind seeks self-definition through relationship with other kinds, and that this search has led us to acknowledge our animal kinship. Is language the boundary of this kinship? Specifically, to what extent does our linguistic prowess make us species-bound?

137

Let us begin by considering the position that language is the glory of humanity. If we believe that language enables the fullest expression of human rationality and creativity, then we incline to the conclusion that we are superior creatures by virtue of possessing the most highly developed linguistic systems, although, interestingly, semiologists estimate that as much as 80 percent of *human* communication is nonverbal. What we derive from the criterion of language, which we have established as the highest governing principle, is confirmation of our supremacy.

Important new evidence on animal cognition and comparative linguistics, too specialized and tentative to be assessed here, is issuing from scientific research. Studies of the sonar transmission of messages among whales and dolphins, the surprising receptivity of primates to learning language from both human instructors and computers, and experiments instructing chimpanzees in gestural language, challenge in as yet inestimable ways traditional notions about our exclusive linguistic capacity.

Even if feelings and emotions can be expressed without highly developed verbal interchange and understanding, what about rational thought? This was the stumbling block for Nietzsche, who, in "The Birth of Tragedy Out of the Spirit of Music," postulates that although music is a primary human expression of the soul, it is also "primitive," because it lacks reason. Are the two terms "skepticism" and "animal faith" really dichotomous, as Santayana's essay proposes?[1] If so, isn't this argument in itself proof that our superiority lies in our linguistic capacity? And what of symbols in mathematics, physics, chemistry, astronomy? Human beings are symbol-creators and symbol-users, a form of communication which perhaps more than anything else distinguishes us from other creatures.

Moreover, human speech itself has been interpreted as a creative act; the fundamental act of Adam's naming the animals is celebrated in dominion's relation. The naming function extends to curses, spells, rhymes of ridicule, and tales of heroic lineage such as the Norse *Eddas*. And what of the overwhelming importance accorded to the name in all legal issues of lineage and property, debates over patronymics and matronymics? What of Lucy Stoners? Pseudonyms? We use language as an instrument through which to secure a place in the historical record, to snatch at a signature that will make us immortal. Edwin Muir's poem "The Day," in which he describes the human race as "Snatched from deceiving death / by the articulate breath" epitomizes this attitude.

Yet this position is less convincing today, when we are accustomed to hear about a generalized breakdown in human communication—between races, generations, nations, genders, expert and nonexpert. The perception of this acute problem provides the title of Adrienne Rich's book on gender difference, *The Dream of a Common Language*. We have learned from political scandal as well as private discourse about "hidden agendas." We have been shown by psychologists how we say one thing with our tongue and simultaneously contradict it with our "body language." Our comprehension has been blunted by the coinage of advertising, the jargon of the media, the impenetrable vocabulary of "experts" who mystify issues by obfuscating the terms of discussion. Academic institutions conduct serious but inconclusive debates about the inclusion of ethnic dialects into the teaching of standard English. And as any translator knows, even without the intention to mislead, it is difficult to understand accurately those who speak in another tongue.

Furthermore, as through technology the political and economic destinies of nations come closer and closer, international failures of communication press in upon us. As we read the newspaper or watch the news on television, dozens of simultaneous wars are reported in which conflict rages but the issues remain unclear.

As a consequence, the Tower of Babel myth, which attempts to provide an explanation for the "falling into many tongues," emerges as a seminal myth for our time, attracting such masterful interpreters as George Steiner (*After Babel*), Reinhold Niebuhr (*Beyond Tragedy*), Jorge Luis Borges (*The Aleph and Other Stories*), Franz Kafka (*Parables*), and Roland Barthes (*The Eiffel Tower, and Other Mythologies*).[2] The word *Babel* itself, in its mutually contradictory definitions, encapsulates the dilemma: its first definition is "gateway to God," its second, "confusion of tongues"—that is, babble.

But the limitations of language need not frustrate all our efforts at relation. There is an equally forceful and traditional conceptualization of language that, while acknowledging the divisiveness of tongues, both among peoples and between human beings and other species, raises basic questions about the alternative powers of silence and nonverbal communication—movement, demeanor, nonverbal sound, gesture, intuition. In Wordsworth's "There Was a Boy" a dialogue is initiated by the boy who:

> Blew mimic hootings to the silent owls,
> That they might answer him . . . with quivering peals,
> And long halloos, and screams, and echoes loud
> Redoubled and redoubled; concourse wild
> Of jocund din

Paradoxically, the written word of poetry has always spoken to the eloquence of silence: Thomas Traherne in the Renaissance declared, "I did lose my bliss when I did silence break," which resembles closely the Eastern mystical wisdom, "The Tao that can be told is not an eternal Tao, the name is not permanent." Similarly, when we assert that we're "left speechless" or we have been "struck dumb" or "words fail us," we express the fact that we feel something stronger, deeper, larger than words can say. In "Less and Less Human, O Savage Spirit," Wallace Stevens pleads for a god not only silent but incapable of speech, one who resembles a silent natural force like "moonlight." Interestingly, Joseph A. Ward, in his study *American Silences*,[3] sees this same viewpoint informing the work of Henry Adams, Melville, Poe, and Henry James, then continuing in artists such as James Agree, Walker Evans, and Edward Hopper—artists, Ward writes, "who denigrated the definitive feature of human life—speech. All three considered verbal expression banal and noxious. The 'word' was not truth, and it did not set us free. . . . In silence, not only were all humans as one, but humans also became reconciled with the remainder of reality. . . . Silence was the vehicle of communion and transcendence."

Communion, in contradistinction to communication, refers to a relation produced through nonverbal, preverbal, or inspired utterance. The power of words to alter or at least influence reality, that is, their magical power, accounts for the idea of secret vocabularies. In Corinthians the ideal is an exalted or revelatory mode described by the phrase "speaking in tongues," a language reserved for prophecy, and totally separated from daily speech. The Pentecostal sects in America today believe in a "glossalalia," or special tongue, in which angels speak.[4] And in the Inuit Eskimo language there are shamanistic words (words only those holy magic-makers may use) for quite everyday things such as *kayak, iglu, turf.* Through the use of this exclusive vocabulary, the shaman is able to intervene in the course of events, "though a literal understanding of the words is quite unnecessary to the singer or his audience."[5] Communion, then, allows not only the possibility of different human relationships, but also the possibility of engagement between the human animal and other animals. As Mircea Eliade writes about human/animal discourse:

> In numerous traditions, friendship with animals and/or understanding their language, represents paradisal syndromes. In the beginning, that is, in mythical times (before the Fall) man lived at peace with animals, and understood their speech.[6]

So believed the Jewish historian Josephus, who added to the list of deprivations coincident upon the expulsion from the Garden the failure of communication among species. Now only the rare spirit, a Saint Francis of Assisi or a Saint Jerome, possesses the gift of this dialogue. In Robert Graves's poem "In The Wilderness," the poet, by picturing Jesus himself communing with a goat and a cockatrice, reveals the value of such embrasiveness.

Western European culture has over the centuries entertained the notion of some primal speech that was lost, a language of nature, instinctual, a word intuiting God's Logos, "a house," as the Mexican writer Octavio Paz phrases it, "common to all." In nonlinguistic terms, this sound has been described as "the music of the spheres," a heavenly harmony understood without recourse to a gloss. After the Fall from the Garden of Eden, Milton characterizes a second fall as a descent into language which is verbal, but divisive:

> Thus they in mutual accusation spent
> the fruitless hours, but neither self-condemning;
> And of their vague contest appear'd no end.

The realization that language may fall short of achieving intimacy prompts Galway Kinnell in "The Waking" to establish a distinction between what he calls "in-the-tongue-language," his term for the special language of communion, and ordinary speech. And his "In the Seekonk Woods" refers to nonverbal language not as a less-developed state, but as something we humans haven't achieved "yet" — a more mature, or higher, order:

> So what if we groan?
> That's our noise. Laughter is our stuttering
> in a language we can't speak yet.

James Dickey shares this view; his poem "A Dog Sleeping on My Feet" voices his regret that he will wake from an animal dream and "fail / Back into the human tongue."

In each case, a recognition of the failure of speech to bring us together or to effect contact with a spiritual power prompts a distinction between communication and communion — secret languages, animal sounds, silence, gestures. Indeed, since we locate a "falling into tongues" as a post-Edenic phenomenon, part of the yearning for a past Golden Age, a lost Eden, is the desire to obviate verbal misunderstanding and arrive at something universal. Both communication and communion are participatory relations, but communion differs from communication in implying intimacy, and especially a spiritual condition of relation.

In Evelyn Waugh's novel *Brideshead Revisited,* Lady Marchmain remarks, a propos of language and communion, "It's not to be expected that an ox and an ass should 'worship' at the crib. Animals are always doing the oddest things in the lives of saints. It's all part of the poetry . . . of religion." And it is the Nativity scene with the animals worshipping at the crib, illustrating the transcendent power of communion, that Thomas Hardy selects as the subject of his poem "The Oxen." Turning on the old country belief that animals are visited by grace once a year on Christmas Eve, the setting of the poem locates the Babe at the center, the animals in the first circle around the manger, with concentric circles of shepherds and kings widening outward. The design is completely inclusive, but with the animals in the closest position to the Child, Hardy echoes the sentiment of the much earlier Christmas carol *"Magnum Mysterium"*: "Who were the first to cry Nowell? / The animals all as it befell."

Hardy's poem, like the carol, pays tribute to the power of communion, which can rise to the holiest understanding without language. Significantly, in Buddhist art of ancient Japan and China, the highly stylized pictures of the death of Buddha, with gods, demigods, trees, animals, humans, oceans, the moon, and Buddha-sun present at the event, unify all the elements of existence into one noble, integrated composition. All have come to witness; neither Buddha nor any person nor any creature nor object of nature in the scrolls *talks*.[7]

Interestingly, in our own time much of the poetic utterance of Roethke, Berryman, Plath, Jarrell, Sexton, and Lowell adopts a persona that is mad, wild, childlike, or hallucinated, the implication being that the writer uncovers realities ordinarily concealed by smooth linear and syntactical structure. Wild speech reveals wild truths. Additionally, the untraditional use of language inaugurated around the time of World War I by Gertrude Stein, Virginia Woolf, Ezra Pound, T. S. Eliot, James Joyce, and others has been pushed to extremes of private idiom by contemporary poets like John Ashbery, Douglas Crase, Norman Dubie, and the French poet Jean Follain. In France the literary movement of surrealism invented a combination of non-sense syllables, DADA, to symbolize the breakdown of traditional language in favor of new juxtapositions, a style practiced, for instance, by contemporary French surrealist poet René Char. Moreover, today there rages an ongoing dispute among linguists, psychologists, and literary critics about the relation of speech to thought, as well as about the parameters of oral and written language. Literary critics like Derrida and Barthes have raised serious doubts about the efficacy of language, calling it an "unstable tool," and emphasizing the impermeability or resistance of experience (things and events) to words. One counterforce to such theories, which have led to the privatization of language, has been the insistence of the "new" Romantic poets like Bly, Creeley, Duncan, and Ginsberg on the importance of the oral tradition, of folk literature, of the Orphic, and of the singing element of poetry. Indeed, Robert Bly frequently accompanies his poetry readings on a dulcimer, Allen Ginsberg on a harmonium.

The poems about communion, then, demonstrate the remarkable way in which our thinking about speech has been turned around. Nowhere in these selections do we read that our verbal tools are the instrument of happiness, or, more surprisingly, of superiority. Quite the contrary, as Lars Gustaffson queries his dog, "Why couldn't I learn from you?" ("Elegy for a Dead Labrador"). As a result of this shift in sentiment, the argument about moral superiority through language is no longer the special province for speculation by the theologian (Bishop Berkeley), or the philosopher (Leibniz), or the linguist (Noam Chomsky); it has become instead the subject matter of a large body of contemporary poetry. These poems share the conviction that the animal's life is organic and wise (even without verbal communication) and that human life is grafted and informational (even with verbal communication). "Dumb" animals are seen not as inferior, but as equal, or even enviable; humans as victims of our own linguistic deceptions. Language, poets say, offers better possibilities for prevarication than any tricks of the wild. As e. e. cummings wrote: "one is the song which fiends and angels sing: / all murdering lies by mortals told make two."

Furthermore, our insistent human effort at transcending both our experiential limitations and our imperfect comprehension of it necessitates enormous responsibilities toward language; in essence, we make our lives more bearable by elevating, interpreting, and improving language as a medium of expression. Animals are to be envied because they do not struggle either to express their condition satisfactorily or to transcend it through shaping utterance. Ironically, too, we know that this very tool, language, at the same time that it serves us as a vehicle of transcendence, is also the means by which we designate our temporality; we are "time's names," says Paz in his poem "Flame, Speech." Other times bring other names: Gaul–France; Saint Petersburg–Leningrad. Language itself is continually evolving and expressing change.

Because language is process, it can describe process in past, future, and conditional tenses, voicing our sense of mutability and potential loss, as well as elegizing what is irrecoverable. The conditional capacity of language poses the "perhaps" of things, the "what if," or alternativity. The poems in Communion assume language to be part of the burden of human materiality. Animals, to the contrary, are not expected to "keep time."

The belief in communion enables the animal/human relationship to transcend difference, reaching into a metalinguistic, more inclusive world. Thus, in Harry Hume's poem "Calling In the Hawk," the man gentles the bird down to him with words; the hawk circles wordlessly, his eyes "blazing with friendship."

From March '79

TOMAS TRANSTRÖMER

Tired of all who come with words, words but no language
I went to the snow-covered island.
The wild does not have words.
The unwritten pages spread themselves out in all
                        directions!
I come across the marks of roe-deer's hooves in the
                        snow.
Language but no words.

translated by John F. Deane

Teaching the Ape to Write

JAMES TATE

They didn't have much trouble
teaching the ape to write poems:
first they strapped him into the chair
then tied his pencil around his hand
(the paper had already been nailed down).
Then Dr. Bluespire leaned over his shoulder
and whispered into his ear:
"You look like a god sitting there.
Why don't you try writing something?"

If the Owl Calls Again

JOHN HAINES

at dusk
from the island in the river,
and it's not too cold,

I'll wait for the moon
to rise,
then take wing and glide
to meet him.

We will not speak,
but hooded against the frost
soar above
the alder flats, searching
with tawny eyes.

And then we'll sit
in the shadowy spruce and
pick the bones
of careless mice,

while the long moon drifts
toward Asia
and the river mutters
in its icy bed.

And when morning climbs
the limbs
we'll part without a sound,
fulfilled, floating
homeward as
the cold world awakens.

Less and Less Human, O Savage Spirit

WALLACE STEVENS

If there must be a god in the house, must be,
Saying things in the rooms and on the stair,

Let him move as the sunlight moves on the floor
Or moonlight, silently, as Plato's ghost

Or Aristotle's skeleton. Let him hang out
His stars on the wall. He must dwell quietly.

He must be incapable of speaking, closed,
As those are: as light, for all its motion, is;

As color, even the closest to us, is;
As shapes, though they portend us, are.

It is the human that is the alien,
The human that has no cousin in the moon.

It is the human that demands his speech
From beasts or from the incommunicable mass.

If there must be a god in the house, let him be one
That will not hear us when we speak: a coolness,

A vermilioned nothingness, any stick of the mass
Of which we are too distantly a part.

Words Rising

ROBERT BLY

I open my journal, write a few
sounds with green ink, and suddenly
fierceness enters me, stars
begin to revolve and pick up
caribou dust from under the ocean.
I see the music, and I feel the bushy
tail of the Great Bear
reach down and brush the seafloor.

All those lives we lived in the sunlit
shelves of the Dordogne, the thousand
tunes we sang to the skeletons
of Papua, the many times
we died wounded under
the cloak of an animal's sniffing,
all of these return, and the grassy
nights we ran for hours in the moonlight.

Watery syllables come welling up.
Anger that barked and howled in the cave,
the luminous head of barley
the priest holds up, growls
from under fur, none of the sounds are lost!
The old earth fragrance remains
in the word "and." We experience
"the," in its lonely suffering.

We are bees then; honey is language.
Honey lies stored in caves
beneath us, and the sounds of words
carry what we do not. When weeping
a man or woman feeds a few words

with private grief, the shames
we knew before we could invent the wheel,
then words grow larger. We slip out

into farmyards, here rabbits lie
stretched out on the ground for buyers.
Wicker baskets and hanged men
come to us as tremors and vowels.
We see a million hands with dusty
palms turned up inside each verb,
lifted. There are eternal vows
held inside the word "Jericho."

Blessings then on the man who labors
in his tiny room, writing stanzas on the lamb;
blessings on the woman, who picks the brown
seeds of solitude out of the black seeds of
        loneliness.
And blessings on the dictionary maker, huddled
        among
his bearded words; and on the setter of songs,
who sleeps at night inside his violin case.

Flame, Speech

OCTAVIO PAZ

I read in a poem:
to talk is divine.
But the gods don't speak:
they make and unmake worlds
while men do the talking.
They play frightening games
without words.

The spirit descends,
loosening tongues,
but doesn't speak words:
it speaks fire.
Lit by a god,
language becomes
a prophecy
of flames and a tower
of smoke and collapse
of syllables burned:
ash without meaning.

The word of man
is the daughter of death.
We talk because we are mortal:
words are not signs, they are years.
Saying what they say,
the words we are saying
say time: they name us.
We are time's names.

To talk is human.

translated by Mark Strand

The Oxen

THOMAS HARDY

Christmas Eve and twelve of the clock.
"Now they are all on their knees,"
An elder said as we sat in a flock
By the embers in hearthside ease.

We pictured the meek mild creatures where
They dwelt in their strawy pen,
How did it occur to one of us there
To doubt they were kneeling then.
So fair a fancy few would weave
In those years! Yet, I feel
If someone said on Christmas Eve,
"Come, see the Oxen kneel

In the lonely barton by yonder coomb
Our childhood used to know,"
I know I should go with him in the gloom,
Hoping it might be so.

St. Francis and the Sow

GALWAY KINNELL

The bud
stands for all things,
even for those things that don't flower,
for everything flowers, from within, of self-blessing;
though sometimes it is necessary
to reteach a thing its loveliness,
to put a hand on its brow
of the flower
and retell it in words and in touch
it is lovely
until it flowers again from within, of self-blessing;
as St. Francis
put his hand on the creased forehead
of the sow, and told her in words and in touch
blessings of earth on the sow, and the sow
began remembering all down her thick length,
from the earthen snout all the way
through the fodder and slops to the spiritual curl of
                the tail,
from the hard spininess spiked out from the spine
down through the great broken heart
to the blue milken dreaminess spurting and shuddering
from the fourteen teats into the fourteen mouths sucking
                and blowing beneath them:
the long, perfect loveliness of sow.

A Dog Sleeping on My Feet

JAMES DICKEY

Being his resting place,
I did not even tense
The muscles of a leg
Or I would seem to be changing.

Remembering what I have written,
Far now, with my feet beneath him
Dying like embers,
The poem is beginning to move
Up through my pine-prickling legs
Out of the night-wood,

Taking hold of the pen by my fingers.
Before me the fox floats lightly,
On fire with his holy scent.
All, all are running.
Marvelous is the pursuit,
Like a dazzle of nails through the ankles,

Like a twisting shout through the trees
Sent after the flying fox
Through the holes of logs, over streams
Stock-still with the pressure of moonlight.
My killed legs,
My legs of a thing, follow.

Quick as pins, in the forest,
And all rushes on into dark
And ends on the brightness of paper.
When my hand, which speaks in a daze
The hypnotized language of beasts,
Shall falter, and fail

Back into the human tongue,
And the dog gets up and goes out
To wander the dawning yard,
I shall crawl to my human bed
And lie there smiling at sunrise,
With the scent of the fox

Burning the brain like incense,
Floating out of the night wood,
Coming home to my wife and sons
From the dream of an animal,
Assembling the self I must wake to,
Sleeping to grow back my legs.

The Song of the Trout-Fisher

IKINILIK

Oft do I return
To my little song.
And patiently I hum it
Above fishing-hole
In the ice.
This simple little song
I can keep on humming
I, who else too quickly
Tire when fishing. Up the stream.

Cold blows the wind
Where I stand on the ice.
I am not long in giving up!
When I get home
With a catch that does not suffice,
I usually say
It was the fish
That failed—
Up the stream.

And yet, glorious is it
To roam
The river's snow-soft ice
As long as my legs care.
Alas! My life has now glided
Far from the wide views of the peaks
Deep down into the vale of age—
Up the stream.

If I go hunting the land-beasts,
Or if I try to fish,

Quickly I fall to my knees,
Stricken with faintness.

Never again shall I feel
The wildness of strength,
When on an errand I go in over land
From my house and those I provide for —
Up the stream.

A worn-out man, that's all,
A fisher, who ever without luck
Makes holes in river or lake-ice
Where no trout will bite.

But life itself is still
So full of goading excitement!
I alone,
I have only my song,
Though it too is slipping from me.

For I am merely
Quite an ordinary hunter,
Who never inherited song
From the twittering birds of the sky.

There Are Things to Be Said

CID CORMAN

There are things to be said. No doubt.
And in one way or another
they will be said. But to whom tell

the silences? With whom share them
now? For a moment the sky is
empty and then there was a bird.

The Owl

EDWARD THOMAS

Down hill I came, hungry, and yet not starved;
Cold, yet had heat within me that was proof
Against the North wind; tired, yet so that rest
Had seemed the sweetest thing under a roof.

Then at the inn I had food, fire and rest,
Knowing how hungry cold and tired was I.
All of the night was quite barred out except
An owl's cry, a most melancholy cry

Shaken out long and clear upon the hill,
No merry note, nor cause of merriment,
But one telling me plain what I escaped
And others could not, that night, as in I went.

And salted was my food, and my repose,
Salted and sobered, too, by the bird's voice
Speaking for all who lay under the stars,
Soldiers and poor, unable to rejoice.

Cleopatra*

BARBARA CHASE-RIBOUD

In
A f r i c a
The strange beasts
Wonder & worry at familiar
Lakes and watch reflections of
Egyptian Gods wade & speak to
Them in a meticulous tongue which is
Not our own nor any we have ever heard
But those who understand it say there is
No sound like their brilliant dialogues
Rustling savannah grass, composing mirages &
Miracle alike with bewildering urgency, as
Urgent as the pressed flesh of our own language
Which might be beautiful if Caesar were in Africa.

*11

Calling In the Hawk

HARRY HUMES

I should have a dead mouse in my hands
on this last day of the year,
and a leather guard the length of my forearm,
for out there on the field's only hickory
is the hawk with its white breast feathers
and its eyes hooking late morning light.
I walk into the field, give out the high whistle,
again and yet again till it shifts on the limb,
one shoulder moving slightly up, one foot restless,
the head looking away, looking back.

Then it drops off, comes low over dry grass
and old barley, flaps slowly, powerfully over briars.
I whistle again. It grows larger,
sets its wings. I raise my right arm.
I see the flaring red tail, the way
feathers hold air like fingers over a balloon,
and there are the nostril slits, the curved beak,
wings tilted, braking, talons tearing
into my arm. It sits there, waiting.

I whisper *pheasant* to it. It leaves my arm,
rises next to clouds, stoops over the orchard,
again comes back low, a great cock
trailing beneath it, comes WHISH to my arm.
I take the pheasant, cook it with wild rice.
The hawk waits someplace else. After wine
I whistle. It comes down through the maples,
lands on the porch. I call it to my bleeding arm.
Good bird, I say, as my dog watches.
Showing off for the woman, I whisper *blue jay.*
It spirals off, comes back. I offer blue

tail feathers for her to weave into the raffia
basket, to wear in her hair, to put into a vase.
She refuses.
                    I am careful not to whisper
fire or *serpent* or *fox trap,* not to whisper
sunspots or *meteor, the depressing distances
of space.* It sits on the scars of my arms
for years. It is pleased I haven't ordered
jess and hood, as it stretches its wings
of February nights. I signal *no,*
that this is the month of sorrow, of dangerous
air heaves, the sink holes by the stream.
The woman piles her baskets in the pantry.
She grows fat, looks at me with distrust,
refuses to pet the bird. One day in March
its head drops, it begins to sleep past noon,
curls up on my arm. The vet thinks accipiter
leukemia, no cure, better to put it down.
So the leg is shaved, the needle inserted.
Outside near the shovel, I whisper, *It happens.*

The next day it is back with something black
happening in its talons, wants to land on my arm.
No, I shout, *Take it back.* I run inside,
hide behind the woman who nurses her child.
It circles the house for days.
I call out *skunk cabbage, spring peeper,
bloodroot, hepatica.* It circles and circles,
talons locked, eyes blazing with friendship.
Through my cupped hands I yell *trout,
long walks, warm rain, the woman naked on the grass.*
It circles the red roof, the grackles building nests.
At last I walk out. It is June, the air
buoyant with thermals. I whistle it down
through the air. It is all familiar.
All afternoon and evening it approaches.
Deep down in my blood something begins.
The final word flaps closer and closer.

FANTASY

"Flying Tiger,"
Chinese, nineteenth century.

*In that countree ben many Griffounes, more plentee
than in any contree. Sum men seyn that thei hand the
Body upward as an Egle, and beneath as a Lyoun: and
treuly thei seyn sothe, that thei ben of that schapp. But
a Griffoun hathe the body more gret and is more strong
than 8 Lyouns; and more gret and strongere than an
100 Egles, such as we han amongst us. For a Griffoun
will bere, fleynge to his Nest, a gret Horse, or 2 Oxen
yoked togider, as thei gon at the Plowghe. For he hathe
his Talouns so longe and so large and grete upon his
Feet, as thoughe thei were Hornes of grete Oxen; so
that men maken cuppes of him, to drynken of; and of
her Ribbes and of the Pennes of hie Wenges, men
maken Bowes fulle stronge, to schote with Arwes and
Quarelle.*

SIR JOHN MANDEVILLE

TRAVELS

*That I may reduce the monster to
Myself, and then may be myself.*

WALLACE STEVENS

"THE MAN WITH THE BLUE GUITAR, XIX"

Whom causes us to invent, create, fantasize about animals that
don't exist? Given the extraordinary range of shapes, colors, sizes,
habits, habitats, furs, skins of creatures to be seen in the real
world, what impulse drives us to add to this munificence?

The obvious answer is that in the past fantastic animals were
the invention of ignorance. There was a time when people believed
in sea monsters and other fanciful creatures because the world
had yet to be traversed, the depths of oceans plumbed, the mountain peaks ascended. We can readily understand how, in the beginning, fantastic creatures were invented to provide explanations
of natural phenomena beyond available human knowledge — the
earthquake was a minotaur rampaging below the ground, fire
the breathing of a dragon. Such explanations can be found in
the histories of Herodotus, Pliny, and Solinus, in Homer and
Hesiod, in the writings of the encyclopedist Isidore of Seville.
Descriptions of fabulous beasts were also passed on through books
of zoology, such as Edward Topsell's *Historie of Foure-Footed
Beasts* and *Historie of Serpents,* published in the Renaissance,
a period that returned to classical literature for inspiration and
instruction. We can trace a literary line of descent from Dante,
in whose *Paradiso* we meet griffins pulling Beatrice's chariot,
through Ariosto to Spenser and Milton.

If this were the only or the complete answer, such invented
creatures would exist only in the literature of the past. However,
in the modern opera *The Unicorn, the Gorgon and the Manticore,*
a social fable about the fickleness of humankind's affection, the
appeal of novelty, and the squandering of gifts, Gian Carlo
Menotti poses this precise question: Why do imaginary creatures
continue to possess the mind?

> If one can stroke the cat and kick the dog;
> If one can pluck the peacock and flee the bee;
> If one can ride the horse and hook the hog;
> If one can tempt the mouse and swat the fly,
> Why, why
> Would a man both rich and well-born
> Raise a unicorn?

If one can strike the boar with the spear
And pierce the lark with an arrow;
If one can hunt the fox and the deer
And net the butterfly and eat the sparrow;
If one can bid the falcon fly and let the robin die
Why, why would a man both rich and well-born
Raise a unicorn?

If one can skin the mole and crush the snake;
If one can tame the swan on the lake
And harpoon the dolphin on the sea;
If one can sport with the monkey and chatter with the
    magpie

Why, why
Would a man both rich and well-born
Raise a unicorn?

For contemporary writing does still invoke the unicorn, the
behemoth, the centaur, the dragon, and other beasts of the imagination. John Gardner, for example, harks back to the eighth-
century story of Beowulf in his novel of the mother-monster,
Grendel; Peter S. Beagle to a vast body of legend in his fantasy
The Unicorn. Given the scarcity today of cultural allusions readers
hold in common, authors may draw more and more upon our
shared, veritably inexhaustible stockpile of animal symbology.
Writers such as Belloc, Borges, Merwin, and T. H. White have
fashioned original, contemporary bestiaries or modern transla-
tions of bestiaries. Such bestiaries as Topsell's jumbled real and
fantastic animals together because the animal lore it drew upon
came from such varied sources as the Bible, superstition, and
painting, in addition to observation. Thus, though bestiaries were
traditionally labeled works of natural history, they were never
scientific; from the start, animals were described in relation to
theology and psychology and symbology. Significantly, recent
bestiaries are no more scientific than their predecessors, and contemporary folklore still conjures up an Abominable Snowman
or a Loch Ness Monster. It seems as though fantastic animals,
of which bestiaries are one expression and individual poems about

imaginary creatures another, must still function for us as the em-
bodiment of another relation apart from reverence, dominion,
fraternity, or communion. Our connections to real animals,
multifarious as they are, would seem to be insufficient to express
everything we feel; animals we fantasize afford us additional scope
for invention, creativity, and, significantly, the integration of emotional impulses.

Many poems about imaginary animals, some of them nonsense verse, are written for children, who are themselves, like
animals, closer to the beginnings of the verbal process; children
invent their own neologisms and constructions, delighted by verbal inventiveness, the forward propulsion of rhythm, and the hyp-
notic repetition of rhyme. Many nonsense words are word combinations, making them resemble not only the neologisms of
childhood, but also fitting them singularly for describing the composite images of which fantastic creatures are formed. Furthermore, children, not yet bound by convention and education, are
open to nonsense, amused by poets like Lewis Carroll, Roald
Dahl, Edward Lear and "The Pobble Without Any Toes." In addition, we can readily project how fantastic animals can quell
childhood's fears. Children experience isolation, have dreams of
conquest, feel the necessity to discover modes of personal survival. Each of these fears finds expression in the tests of *Alice
in Wonderland*. Think of Alice faced with the disquieting and
inexplicable appearance and disappearance of the Cheshire cat,
or the Snark who devours the baker, or the Jabberwocky, who
must be slain. The apprehensions of childhood are reinforced by
the fact that children's perception of the line between reality and
unreality is much less rigid than adults'. Children have nightmares,
know there are wild things. All the more reason to consign
threatening apparitions to an invented, remote place; *Where the
Wild Things Are*[1] means they are not *here*. When Jules Verne's
submarine *Nautilus* does battle with a giant octopus, this scari-
fying event occurs at *Twenty Thousand Leagues Under the Sea*.

For adults, these fantastic creations, often animal/animal
combinations or human/animal combinations, fulfill a different
function than symbolic or emblematic animals which are simplifi-

cations do, the isolation of a specific trait from the diversity of being. Fantastic animals enable us to portray complication and conflict by embodying them in forms especially invented for the purpose. Tension between what we wish to repress and what we wish to express may account for the paradoxes of composite morphology and divided nature, as in the satyr—half-goat, half-man. Incorporating the goat's randiness (satyriasis), symbolized by hairy skin and hooves, this being's upper half, the human torso, is playing a pipe, that is, capable of art. Literature and the visual arts inform us that the unicorn, one of the most enduring of imaginative creatures, always white, is emblematic of sexual purity, and hence will rest its head only on the lap of a virgin. We cannot overlook, however, the contradiction apparent to our own eyes, namely the long, pointed, phallic horn and the goatlike beard. The paradoxical combination of purity and sexuality leads Jung to see the unicorn as hermaphroditic, representing "spiritual fecundity."[2] Interestingly, books on animal lore reveal that originally the unicorn was not a symbol of purity; it has been converted into one only in comparatively recent times.

Fantastic animals can embody qualities we may not wish or need to internalize, as we may wish to "put on" the strength of the lion, the fleetness of the deer, the purity of the lamb, the majesty and ferocity of the jaguar. The chimeras of our own imagination often feel uncanny, even frighteningly powerful in the absence of confirming observation and objective correlatives. Thus, in "A Difference of Zoos," Gregory Corso describes the subjective, imaginary zoo created by his mind as "unbearable," and concludes the poem, "and oh thank God for the simple elephant." Fantastic creatures may arise from an earlier world of demonology, subliminally felt, now lost as common reference. After all, do we not fashion Satan still with the cloven hooves and tail of an animal, the swooping wings of a bat? Imaginary creatures are the creations of our dreams, or nightmares, and their significance is often as complicated and shadowy as dream protagonists are, like the monsters who throng the last pages of Flaubert's *The Temptation of Saint Anthony*. For both adults and children, fantasy may serve to distance fears about our own bodies, projections of injury, absence, change, or even death. Violeta Parra directs a diatribe at death by asserting its monstrosity: "Death is an animal . . . / this cannibal of a Satan," "a whirlwind twister," "a grinder," "a killer shark," a "tough old bird" with "slashing claws."

While none of these phrases by itself describes a fantastic animal, their combination in one creature does. Death, most to be feared, is personified as an animal, but not a recognizable one. No one animal is powerful enough to portray this irresistible force, "too terrible to withstand."

Indeed, imaginary animals may be created to subjugate, or at least give voice to the overwhelming and the unknown. Thus, W. B. Yeats, in his apocalyptic poem "The Second Coming," conveys terror at the breakdown of the civilized world by figuring forth dark forces in the frightening image of a man/animal, a moving sphinx. Here not only is the form of the beast compound, but its threat is compounded by showing it moving inexorably toward us, rather than maintaining its traditional static posture upon the sand:

> The Second Coming! Hardly are those words out
> When a vast image out of *Spiritus Mundi*
> Troubles my sight: somewhere in the sands of the desert
> A shape with lion body and the head of a man,
> A gaze blank and pitiless as the sun,
> Is moving its slow thighs, while all about it
> Reel shadows of the indignant desert birds.

The timeless human yearning for magic and mystery, which is in itself the desire for a superhuman, controlling force of deliverance from unseen malevolence, leads a twentieth-century Japanese poet still to fashion twilight on Mount Fuji in the lineaments of a dragon, whom he implores:

> Why should the ways of the world be sad?
> . . .
> Sharp eyes, sharp claws, close them, close them—

The dragon, historically a destructive personification, is held responsible in different cultures for causing an eclipse by swallowing the sun, for feeding on young maidens, for scorching the earth with its hot breath. The contemporary prayer for mercy in the lines above is addressed to the same traditional personification of evil force.

Creatures of our own imagining are, perhaps, extreme attempts to integrate the conflicts and untidiness of human nature, combining paganism and piety, love and hate, humaneness and brutality, science and magic in wholly new, multivalent shapes.

This Is the Creature

RAINER MARIA RILKE

Oh this beast is the one never was.
They didn't know that; unconcerned, they had
loved its grace, its walk, and how it stood
looking at them calmly, with clear eyes.

It hadn't *been*. But from their love, a pure
beast arose. They always left it room.
And in that heart-space, radiant and bare,
it raised its head and hardly needed to

exist. They fed it, not with any grain,
but always just with the thought that it might be.
And this assurance gave the beast so much power,

it grew a horn upon its brow. One horn.
Afterward it approached a virgin, whitely—
and was, inside the mirror and in her.

translated by Stephen Mitchell

Leviathan

W. S. MERWIN

This is the black sea-brute bulling through wave-wrack,
Ancient as ocean's shifting hills, who in sea-toils
Travelling, who furrowing the salt acres
Heavily, his wake hoary behind him,
Shoulders spouting, the fist of his forehead
Over wastes gray-green crashing, among horses unbroken
From bellowing fields, past bone-wreck of vessels,
Tide-ruin, wash of lost bodies bobbing
No longer sought for, and islands of ice gleaming,
Who ravening the rank flood, wave marshalling,
Overmastering the dark sea-marches, find home
And harvest. Frightening to foolhardiest
Mariners, his size were difficult to describe:
The hulk of him is like hills heaving,
Dark, yet as crags of drift-ice, crowns cracking in thunder,
Like land's self by night black-looming, surf churning and
    trailing
Along his shores' rushing, shoal-water boding
About the dark of his jaws; and who should moor at his
    edge
And fare on afoot would find no gates of no gardens,
But the hill of dark underfoot diving,
Closing overhead, the cold deep, and drowning.
He is called Leviathan, and named for rolling,
First created he was of all creatures,
He has held Jonah three days and nights,
He is that curling serpent that in ocean is,
Sea-fright he is, and the shadow under the earth.
Days there are, nonetheless, when he lies
Like an angel, though a lost angel
On the waste's unease, no eye of man moving,
Bird hovering, fish flashing, creature whatever

Who after him came to herit the earth's emptiness.
Froth at flanks seething soothes to stillness,
Waits; with one eye he watches
Dark of night sinking last, with one eye dayrise
As at first over foaming pastures. He makes no cry
Though that light is a breath. The sea curling,
Star-limbed, wind-combed, cumbered with itself still
As at first it was, is the hand not yet contented
Of the Creator. And he waits for the world to begin.

The Origin of Centaurs
for Dimitri Hadzi

ANTHONY HECHT

But to the girdle do the gods inherit,
Beneath is all the fiends.
                    —King Lear

This mild September mist recalls the soul
                To its own lust;
            On the enchanted lawn
It sees the iron top of the flagpole
            Sublimed away and gone
Into Parnassian regions beyond rust;
And would undo the body to less than dust.

Sundial and juniper have been dispelled
                Into thin air.
            The pale ghost of a leaf
Haunts those uncanny softnesses that felled
            And whitely brought to grief
The trees that only yesterday were there.
The soul recoils into its own despair,

Knowing that though the horizon is at hand,
                Twelve paltry feet
            Refuse to be traversed,
And form themselves before wherever you stand
            As if you were accursed;
While stones drift from the field, and the arbor-seat
Floats toward some millefleurs world of summer heat.

Yet from the void where the azalea bush
                Departed hence,

Sadly the soul must hear
Twitter and cricket where should be all hush,
    And from the belvedere
A muffled grunt survives in evidence
That love must sweat under the weight of sense.

Or so once thought a man in a Greek mist—
        Who set aside
    The wine-cup and the wine,
And the deep fissure he alone had kissed,
        All circumscribing line,
Moved to the very edge in one swift stride
And took those shawls of nothing for his bride.

Was it the Goddess herself? Some dense embrace
        Closed like a bath
    Of love about his head;
Perfectly silent and without a face.
        Blindfolded on her bed,
He could see nothing but the aftermath:
Those powerful, clear hoofprints on the path.

The Man-Moth

ELIZABETH BISHOP

Here, above,
cracks in the buildings are filled with battered moonlight.
The whole shadow of Man is only as big as his hat.
It lies at his feet like a circle for a doll to stand on,
and he makes an inverted pin, the point magnetized to the moon.
He does not see the moon; he observes only her vast properties,
feeling the queer light on his hands, neither warm nor cold,
of a temperature impossible to record in thermometers.

But when the Man-Moth
pays his rare, although occasional, visits to the surface,
the moon looks rather different to him. He emerges
from an opening under the edge of one of the sidewalks
and nervously begins to scale the faces of the buildings.
He thinks the moon is a small hole at the top of the sky,
proving the sky quite useless for protection.
He trembles, but must investigate as high as he can climb.

Up the facades,
his shadow dragging like a photographer's cloth behind him,
he climbs fearfully, thinking this time he will manage
to push his small head through that round clean opening
and be forced through, as from a tube, in black scrolls on
      the light.
(Man, standing below him, has no such illusions.)
But what the Man-Moth fears most he must do, although
he fails, of course, and falls back scared but quite unhurt.

Then he returns
to the pale subways of cement he calls his home. He flits,
he flutters, and cannot get aboard the silent trains
fast enough to suit him. The doors close swiftly.

179

The Man-Moth always seats himself facing the wrong way
and the train starts at once at its full, terrible speed,
without a shift in gears or a gradation of any sort.
He cannot tell the rate at which he travels backwards.

                          Each night he must
be carried through artificial tunnels and dream recurrent dreams.
Just as the ties recur beneath his train, these underlie
his rushing brain. He does not dare to look out the window,
for the third rail, the unbroken draught of poison,
runs there beside him. He regards it as a disease
he has inherited the susceptibility to. He has to keep
his hands in his pockets, as others must wear mufflers.

                        If you catch him,
hold up a flashlight to his eye. It's all dark pupil,
an entire night itself, whose haired horizon tightens
as he stares back, and closes up the eye. Then from the lids
one tear, his only possession, like the bee's sting, slips.
Slyly he palms it, and if you're not paying attention
he'll swallow it. However, if you watch, he'll hand it over,
cool as from underground springs and pure enough to drink.

Dreamtigers

JORGE LUIS BORGES

In my childhood I was a fervent worshipper of the tiger: not the
jaguar, the spotted 'tiger' of the Amazonian tangles and
the isles of vegetation that float down the Parana, but that
striped, Asiatic, royal tiger, that can be faced only by a man
of war, on a castle atop an elephant. I used to linger endlessly
before one of the cages at the zoo; I judged vast encyclopedias
and books of natural history by the splendor of their tigers.
(I still remember those illustrations: I who cannot rightly
recall the brow or the smile of a woman.) Childhood passed
away, and the tigers and my passion for them grew old, but still
they are in my dreams. At that submerged or chaotic level
they keep prevailing. And so, as I sleep, some dream beguiles me,
and suddenly I know I am dreaming. Then I think: This is a dream,
a pure diversion of my will; and now that I have unlimited power,
I am going to cause a tiger.

Oh, incompetence! Never can my dreams engender the wild
    beast I
long for. The tiger indeed appears, but stuffed or flimsy, or
with impure variations of shape, or of an implausible size, or
all too fleeting, or with a touch of the dog or the bird.

The Beast

MARIE HOWE

When I ask her what it sounds like
she says it grunts, it drools,

it's hunched over and grinning.
When I ask her who it is, she says it's her.

When I look her in the eye and ask, is it talking
to me now? Is the beast talking when you talk?

She thinks for a minute, and says, no, it's curled up.
She's talking, but it's watching her.

Later that night, I make love for hours,
I forget my name, where my arms are, what

my tongue is doing. I think I must have cried out
unimaginable things and I think of my sister

in the next room, lying on her back, blinking in the dark.
The next morning, we make coffee and talk about the beast
    again.

My sister is rinsing out her cup when she turns
and says, slowly, it's *male* you know.

She looks surprised.

Death Is an Animal

VIOLETA PARRA

Death is an animal
relentless, fine and high
rowdy and spoiling for a fight:
nothing like her anywhere.
When she shows her head
suddenly it's cold as ice
a mysterious moaning
comes out of her throat
there's a sense of fear
too terrible to withstand.

She comes like a whirlwind twister
striking sparks from the ground
no matter if you think you're divine
you'll never escape her greed.
Her teeth are a grinder
that feeds on mortal flesh
this cannibal of a Satan
dwells on every horizon,
every lowland and mountain,
death is an animal.

No force on earth can stop her
once she's set her eyes on you,
passed by and sunk her hooks in
no wind on earth can stop her.
No use screaming or ranting
or trying to pay her off,
no ifs, ands, or buts about it
I'm telling you for sure,
death is a killer shark
tragic and fine and high.

There's no counting up her damage
no number can be given
to tell how many victims
she's folded into her bed.
Sound- or feeble-bodied,
grumblers and flatterers,
freemen and prisoners,
peacemakers, chatterers,
cowards and wrong-righters,
madmen and fight-pickers.

Against this furious animal
no learned man can prevail
his studying won't help him
nor will a famous name
nor will a fancy title
they're all chucked into the grave
there's nobody like this tough old bird
for snatching what grabs her fancy
and the sneaky skeleton goes around
like butter won't melt in her mouth.

Don't give me death, not even
served up on a silver platter
from out of the graveyard she strikes
with a swipe of her slashing claws
My dear, I don't care to see you
even at the Resurrection
I lay my curse upon you
for you to cut your hair
with Lucifer up in the heavens
and down in his fiery furnace.

translated by Naomi Lindstrom

A Difference of Zoos

GREGORY CORSO

I went to the Hotel Broog;
and it was there I imagined myself singing *Ave Maria*
    to a bunch of hoary ligneous Brownies.
I believe in gnomes, in midges;
I believe to convert the bogeyman,
take Medusa to Kenneth's;
beg Zeus Polyphemus a new eye;
and I thanked all the men who ever lived,
thanked life the world
    for the chimera, the gargoyle,
    the sphinx, the griffin,
    Rumpelstiltskin —
I sang *Ave Maria*
for the Heap, for Groot,
for the mugwump, for Thoth,
the centaur, Pan;
I summoned them all into my room in the Broog,
the werewolf, the vampire, Frankenstein,
every monster imaginable
and sang and sang *Ave Maria* —
The room got to be unbearable!
I went to the zoo
and oh thank God for the simple elephant.

The Grove

EDWIN MUIR

There was no road at all to that high place
But through the smothering grove,
Where as we went the shadows wove
Adulterous shapes of animal hate and love,
The idol-crowded nightmare Space,
Wood beyond wood, tree behind tree,
And every tree an empty face
Gashed by the casual lightning mark
The first great Luciferian animal
Scored on leaf and bark.
This was, we knew, the heraldic ground,
And therefore now we heard our footsteps fall
With the true legendary sound,
Like secret trampling behind a wall,
As if they were saying: To be: to be.

And oh the silence, the drugged thicket dozing
Deep in its dream of fear,
The ring closing
And coming near,
The well-bred self-sufficient animals
With clean rank pelts and proud and fetid breath,
Screaming their arrogant calls,
Their moonstone eyes set straight at life and
    death.
Did we see or dream it? And the jungle cities—
For there were cities here and civilizations
Deep in the forest; powers and dominations
Like shapes begotten by dreaming animals,
Profound animal dreams uplifted high,
Booted and saddled on the animal's back
And staring with the arrogant animal's eye:

186

The golden dukes, the silver earls, and gleaming
    black
The curvetting knights sitting their curvetting
    steeds,
The sweet silk-tunicked eunuchs singing ditties,
Swaying like wandering weeds,
The scarlet cardinals,
And lions high in the air on the banner's field,
Crowns, sceptres, spears and stars and moons of
    blood,
And sylvan wars in bronze within the shield,
All quartered in the wide world's wood,
The smothering grove where there was place for
    pities.

We trod the maze like horses in a mill,
And then passed through it
As in a dream of the will.
How could it be? There was the stifling grove,
Yet here was light; what wonder led us to it?
How could the blind path go
To climb the crag and top the towering hill,
And all that splendour spread? We know
There was no road except the smothering grove.

Mount Fuji, Opus 5

KUSANO SHIMPEI

Flame of fire mountain
Reflecting red in the snow,
Gentle flame, reflecting on the snow's shoulder,
Flame, standing calmly in the sky,
Snuffed in the thick of night.

Look, there above it,
Straight above it, among the open spaces on the moon,
Its great spirals, winds a blue-green cord.

Drawing near,
I would ask the dragon:

"Why should the ways of the world be sad?
Let the swirling clouds coil no longer,
Let the flames dazzle from your glittering scales . . .
Lula-lula-la —
Sharp eyes, sharp claws, close them, close them —
Lula-lula-la — See how it coils!"

The Second Coming

W. B. YEATS

Turning and turning in the widening gyre
The falcon cannot hear the falconer;
Things fall apart; the centre cannot hold;
Mere anarchy is loosed upon the world,
The blood-dimmed tide is loosed, and everywhere
The ceremony of innocence is drowned;
The best lack all conviction, while the worst
Are full of passionate intensity.

Surely some revelation is at hand;
Surely the Second Coming is at hand.
The Second Coming! Hardly are those words out
When a vast image out of *Spiritus Mundi*
Troubles my sight: somewhere in the sands of the desert
A shape with lion body and the head of a man,
A gaze blank and pitiless as the sun,
Is moving its slow thighs, while all about it
Reel shadows of the indignant desert birds.
The darkness drops again; but now I know
That twenty centuries of stony sleep
Were vexed to nightmare by a rocking cradle,
And what rough beast, its hour come round at last,
Slouches towards Bethlehem to be born?

CONCLUSION

The major purpose of this book has been to show that all our imaginative relationships with animals are expressions of the perpetual human desire for self-knowledge, and that animals offer a unique instrument for this quest.

Although the physical sciences have provided new and revolutionary explanations of matter, these answers do not provide an understanding of our *human* nature, its essence, its differentness. The larger cosmic proposals of physics, astronomy, mathematics impart ways of understanding we cannot visualize or, for the most part, even conceptualize. How can we stand toward a cosmos of forces and laws except in a detached and literally distant relation? And the tangible tools of technology have proven no more useful for explaining ourselves to ourselves than have the theoretical laws of the cosmos. Our daily lives, both at work and at home, are filled with mechanical objects and technological devices which in many instances replace the animal, but, unlike the animal, these inanimates cannot stand as analogues to humankind. Our own products cannot be our "other." Indeed, such a prospect is frightening enough to turn us toward living counterparts.

We have always defined ourselves by comparison with other creatures, and we still do so today. How can the machine offer us perspective on the question posed by the Psalmist, asked anew by each generation out of its own circumstantial web: "What is man that Thou art mindful of him?" That question poses depths of both uniqueness and relatedness to which the object is irrele-

190

vant. We seek, perforce, a relation to likeness. As the contemporary Bulgarian poet Nicolai Kantchev expresses it, "I've not given myself to machines so much / I can't see that the firmament's eyelash is a bird's feather."[1]

Because literature keeps animals—past, present, mythic—alive to us, it is a crucial part of our effort to locate ourselves in the created world. By thinking about ourselves and animals in a relational, comparative way, we gain some intimation of what *we* are. We use them to feel at home in the world.

From pre-Biblical times to the present moment, the relationships encoded in poetry belong to an "eternal present"—they are timeless expressions of our human connectedness to the animal kingdom. In literature we discover how we invent and reinvent our animals to help us understand our own mystery.

NOTES

Introduction

1. William Severini Kowinski, *The Malling of America* (New York: William Morrow, 1985). For other books on this subject, see also René Dubos and Barbara Ward, *Only One Earth* (New York: W. W. Norton & Co., 1972); *The Environmental Crisis,* edited by Harold W. Helfrich, Jr. (New Haven and London: Yale University Press, 1970); *This Little Planet,* edited by Michael Hamilton (New York: Charles Scribner's Sons, 1970).

2. Alvin Toffler, *Future Shock* (New York: Random House, 1970).

Reverence

1. Helen Vendler, *The New York Review of Books,* Oct. 23, 1986, 49.

2. For a discussion of this point, see Barry Lopez, *Arctic Dreams* (New York: Bantam Books, 1987).

3. W. H. Auden, "Two Bestiaries" in *The Dyer's Hand* (New York: Random House, 1948).

4. John Berger, *On Seeing* (New York: Pantheon Books, 1980).

5. Virgil, *The Aeneid,* translated by Robert Fitzgerald (New York: Random House, 1980).

6. Cavafy, "The Horses of Achilles," in *The Complete Poems of Cavafy,* translated by Rae Dalven (New York, San Diego, London: Harcourt Brace Jovanovich, 1961).

Dominion

1. Bruce Chatwin, *The Songlines* (New York: Viking, Elizabeth Sifton Books, 1987).

2. Jonathan Schell, *The Fate of the Earth* (New York: Knopf, 1982).

3. See, among others: Jane Goodall, *The Chimpanzees of Zombe: Patterns of Behavior* (Cambridge, Mass.: Harvard University Press, 1987).

Fraternity

1. See bibliography.

2. Vincent Brian Wigglesworth, *The Life of Insects* (Cleveland: World Publishing Co., 1964, reprint).

3. Konrad Lorenz, *On Aggression,* translated by Marjorie Kerr Wilson (New York: Harcourt Brace & World, 1966).

4. For fictional examples of the extra dimensions such metamorphosis affords the reader, see Elizabeth Marshall Thomas, *Reindeer Moon* (Boston: Houghton Mifflin, 1987) and the conclusion of Margaret Atwood, *Surfacing* (New York: Bantam Books, 1987).

5. Charles Robert Darwin, *The Expression of the Emotions in Man and Animals* (New York: Appleton, 1873. Reprint: Philosophical Library, 1955).

6. Art Spiegelman, *Maus: A Survivor's Tale* (New York: Pantheon Books, 1986).

7. For a full account of this bond, see Margaret Joan Blount, *Animal Land: The Creation of Children's Fiction* (New York: William Morrow, 1975).

8. See Stith Thompson, *Index of Folk Literature* (Bloomington: University of Indiana Press, 1932).

9. For a detailed discussion of the human/pet relationship, see Alan Beck and Aaron Katcher, *Between Pets and People: The Importance of Animal Companionship* (New York: G. P. Putnam's Sons, 1983) and James Serpell, *The Company of Animals: A Study of Human-Animal Relationships* (London: Basil Blackwell, 1987).

Communion

1. George Santayana, *Animal Faith and Spiritual Life: Previously Unpublished and Uncollected Writings,* with critical essays on his thought, edited by John Lacks (New York: Appleton, 1967).

2. See bibliography.

3. Joseph Ward, *American Silences: The Realism of James Agee, Walker Evans, and Edward Hopper* (Baton Rouge: Louisiana State University Press, 1985).

4. William J. Samarin, *Tongues of Men and Angels* (New York: Macmillan, 1972).

5. Robert Columbo, ed., *Poems of the Inuit* (Ottawa, Canada: Oberon Press, 1981).

6. Mircea Eliade, *Myth and Reality* (New York: Harper & Row, 1963).

7. Philip Kapleau, "Animals," *Parabola Magazine,* vol. VIII, no. 2:75.

Fantasy

1. Maurice Sendak, *Where the Wild Things Are* (New York: Harper & Row, 1964).

2. Quoted by Rob Baker, "The Persistence of Unicorns," *Parabola Magazine,* vol. VIII, no. 2:91.

Conclusion

1. Nicolai Kantchev, "Telling It," *Medusa, Selected Poems, The Quarterly Review of Literature,* vol. XXXVI (1986): 31.

Selected Prose Bibliography

Aeschylus. *The Oresteia.* Translated by Robert Fagles. New York: Viking, 1975.

Auden, W. H. "Two Bestiaries," in *The Dyer's Hand.* New York: Random House, 1962.

Barthes, Roland. *The Eiffel Tower, and Other Mythologies.* Translated by Richard Howard. New York: Hill & Wang, 1979.

Beck, Alan, and Katcher, Aaron. *Between Pets and People: The Importance of Animal Companionship.* New York: Putnam, 1983.

Berger, John. *About Looking.* New York: Pantheon Books, 1980.

Bettelheim, Bruno. *The Uses of Enchantment: The Meaning and Importance of Fairy Tales.* New York: Knopf, 1976.

Blount, Margaret Joan. *Animal Land: The Creation of Children's Fiction.* New York: William Morrow, 1975.

Borges, Jorge Luis. *The Aleph and Other Stories, 1939–1969.* Translated by Norman Thomas di Giovanni. New York: Dutton, 1970.

Briggs, Katharine. *British Folk Tales.* New York: Pantheon Books, 1977.

Byrne, St. Claire, ed. *The Elizabethan Zoo.* Boston: David Godine, 1979.

Chatwin, Bruce. *The Songlines.* New York: Viking, 1987.

Clark, Kenneth. *Animals and Men.* New York: William Morrow, 1977.

Darwin, Charles Robert. *The Expression of the Emotions in Man and Animals.* New York: Appleton, 1873. Reprint. Philosophical Library, 1955.

de Cirrieux, Marc. *Watunna: An Orinoco Creation Cycle.* Translated by David M. Guss. Berkeley: North Point Press, 1980.

Eliade, Mircea. *Myth and Reality.* Translated by Willard R. Trask. New York: Harper & Row, 1963.

Empson, William. *Some Versions of Pastoral.* New York: New Directions, 1974.

Euripides. *The Bacchae and Other Plays.* Translated by Philip Vellacott. New York: Penguin, 1972.

Fisher, M. F. K. *A Cordiall Water.* Berkeley: North Point Press, 1981.

Fox, Michael. *Between Animal and Man.* New York: Coward, McCann & Geoghegan, 1979.

Fox, Michael, and Morris, Richard Knowles, eds. *On The Fifth Day.* Washington, D.C.: Acropolis Press, 1978.

Hearne, Vicki. *Adam's Task.* New York: Knopf, 1982.

Helfrich, Harold W., Jr., ed. *The Environmental Crisis: Man's Struggle to Live with Himself.* New Haven: Yale University Press, 1970.

Hesiod. *Works and Days.* London: Penguin, 1973.

Jones, Richard, and Daniels, Kate, eds. *Of Solitude and Silence.* Boston: Beacon Press, 1981.

Jung, Carl Gustav. *Man and His Symbols.* Garden City, N.Y.: Doubleday, 1964.

Kafka, Franz. *Parables and Paradoxes in German and English.* New York: Schocken Books, 1961.

Klaits, Joseph, and Klaits, Barrie, eds. *Animals and Man in Historical Perspective.* New York: Harper & Row, 1974.

Kowinski, William Severini. *The Malling of America.* New York: William Morrow, 1985.

Leiss, William. *The Domination of Nature.* Boston: Beacon Press, 1972.

Lopez, Barry. *Of Wolves and Men.* New York: Charles Scribner's Sons, 1978.

———. *Arctic Dreams.* New York: Charles Scribner's Sons, 1986.

Lorenz, Konrad. *On Aggression.* Translated by Marjorie Kerr Wilson. New York: Harcourt Brace & World, 1966.

Lovejoy, Arthur. *The Great Chain of Being.* Cambridge, Mass.: Harvard University Press, 1976.

Mandeville, Sir John. *Voyages and Travels.* Edited by Arthur Layard, with a critical and biographical introduction by James W. Redway. New York: Appleton, 1899.

Marx, Leo. *The Machine in the Garden.* New York: Oxford University Press, 1964.

Midgley, Mary. *Animals and Why They Matter.* Athens, Ga.: University of Georgia Press, 1983.

Niebuhr, Reinhold. *Beyond Tragedy; Essays on the Christian Interpretation of History.* New York: Charles Scribner's Sons, 1937.

Novak, Barbara. *Nature and Culture.* New York: Oxford University Press, 1980.

Paz, Octavio. *The Monkey Grammarian.* Translated by Helen R. Lane. New York: Seaver Books, 1981.

Rowland, Beryl. *Animals with Human Faces.* Knoxville, Tenn.: University of Tennessee Press, 1973.

Sagan, Carl. *The Dragons of Eden.* New York: Random House, 1977.

Sale, Roger. *Fairy Tales and After.* Cambridge, Mass.: Harvard University Press, 1978.

Samarin, William J. *Tongues of Men and Angels.* New York: Macmillan, 1972.

Santayana, George. *Animal Faith and Spiritual Life: Previously Unpublished and Uncollected Writings,* with critical essays on his thought. Edited by John Lacks. New York: Appleton, 1967.

Schell, Jonathan. *The Fate of the Earth.* New York: Knopf, 1982.

Serpell, James. *In the Company of Animals: A Study of Human-Animal Relationships.* London: Basil Blackwell, 1987.

Spiegelman, Art. *Maus: A Survivor's Tale.* New York: Pantheon Books, 1986.

Steiner, George. *After Babel.* New York: Oxford University Press, 1975.

Thomas, Elizabeth Marshall. *Reindeer Moon.* Boston: Houghton Mifflin, 1987.

Thomas, Keith. *Man and the Natural World.* New York: Pantheon Books, 1983.

Toffler, Alvin. *Future Shock.* New York: Random House, 1970.

Wagner, Richard H. *Environment and Man.* New York: Norton, 1971.

Ward, Joseph. *American Silences: The Realism of James Agee, Walker Evans, and Edward Hopper.* Baton Rouge: Louisiana State University Press, 1985.

Index to Poems

DATE DUE

MAY 1 7 99 X			
JAN 2 3 1999			
MAY 1 5 '00 S			
APR 2 6 2000			
GAYLORD			PRINTED IN U.S.A.